Vanna's Favorite Crochet Gifts

©2001 by Oxmoor House, Inc.
Book Division of Southern Progress Corporation
P.O. Box 2463, Birmingham, Alabama 35201

Published by Oxmoor House, Inc., and Leisure Arts, Inc.

Library of Congress Catalog Number: 2001 132273
Hardcover ISBN: 0-8487-2451-8
Softcover ISBN: 0-8487-2452-6
Printed in the United States of America
First Printing 2001

Editor-in-Chief: Nancy Fitzpatrick Wyatt
Executive Editor: Susan Carlisle Payne
Senior Crafts Editor: Susan Ramey Cleveland
Senior Editor, Editorial Services: Olivia Kindig Wells
Art Director: Cynthia R. Cooper

Vanna's Favorite Crochet Gifts

Editor: Catherine Corbett Fowler
Copy Editor: L. Amanda Owens
Contributing Technical Copy Editor: Patty Kowaleski
Editorial Assistant: Suzanne Powell
Contributing Designer: Rita A. Yerby
Director, Production and Distribution: Phillip Lee
Production Coordinator: Leslie Wells Johnson
Senior Photographer: Jim Bathie
Photographers: Ralph Anderson, Brit Huckabay
Photo Stylist: Kay Clarke
Publishing Systems Administrator: Rick Tucker
Illustrator: Kelly Davis

We're Here for You!

We at Oxmoor House are dedicated to serving you with reliable information that expands your imagination and enriches your life. We welcome your comments and suggestions. Please write us at:

Oxmoor House, Inc.
Editor, *Vanna's Favorite Crochet Gifts*
2100 Lakeshore Drive
Birmingham, AL 35209

To order additional publications, call 1-800-633-4910.

For more books to enrich your life, visit
oxmoorhouse.com

Contents

Introduction

Welcome to *Vanna's Favorite Crochet Gifts*—my fourth book of gorgeous crocheted items! Lots of changes have taken place in my life since my last crochet book: My family and I moved into a new house, and I'm happy to say it is really beginning to feel like home. In fact, the colors and the decorating styles in our new place inspired some of the projects in this publication.

And you're sure to notice how much my son, Nikko, and my daughter, Giovanna, have grown since my last book. They were both good sports and agreed to model some of the projects featured on the upcoming pages. I also have a new nephew. He can certainly move quickly, but we were able to catch him for one photograph. You'll find him enjoying the "Playful Plaid" pallet on page 73. Despite all the changes, one area of my life has remained constant: my love for crochet.

For whatever the celebration, you'll find me planning a beautiful hand-crocheted gift. With that in mind, I'm thrilled to present this collection of more than 45 present-perfect crocheted items.

In *Vanna's Favorite Crochet Gifts*, I worked with Oxmoor House and David Blumenthal, senior vice

> *"... one area of my life has remained constant: my love for crochet."*

president and chief operating officer of Lion Brand Yarn Company, to bring you all-new designs, including 31 never-before-published afghans. There are some small afghans and simple patterns that work up quickly, if time is important. And there are also some heirloom-quality pieces, for those truly special occasions.

But I realize there's more to crochet than afghans, so I feature other items for your home—such as a frame, a wreath, a stocking, a pillow, and even Christmas ornaments.

And since fashion is such a big part of my life, I thought it would be fun to develop easy, yet attractive apparel designs. Thanks to all of the fabulous styles, textures, and colors of Lion Brand yarns, we were able to do just that! In this collection, you'll find a wide range of women's and children's clothing. From a wrap to a purse, from slippers to sweaters, from tunics to coats, you're bound to find something wonderful for your wardrobe.

So take a few minutes and browse through our patterns. I'm sure you'll discover lots of gift items to fit whichever occasion is just around the corner.

Vanna White

Warm Up America!

This afghan will warm a heart as well as a lap. Designed to the specifications of Warm Up America!™ (see page 8 for details), these blocks work up quickly into a cozy coverlet. Make one for a friend and then stitch a few extra rectangles—or perhaps an entire afghan—for this charitable organization.

MATERIALS

Chunky-weight yarn, approximately:
18 oz. (555 yd.) purple, MC
18 oz. (555 yd.) brown, A
12 oz. (370 yd.) teal, B
18 oz. (555 yd.) variegated, C
Size J crochet hook or size to obtain gauge
Yarn needle

FINISHED SIZE

Approximately 49" x 63"

GAUGE

Ea Rectangle = 7" x 9"

SHELL NETWORK RECTANGLE

(Make 7.)
With MC, ch 25.

Row 1 (rs): 5 dc in 6th ch from hook, * skip next 2 chs, dc in next ch **, ch 1, skip next ch, dc in next ch, skip next 2 chs, 5 dc in next ch; rep from * across, ending last rep at **.
Note: *Mark last row as rs.*
Row 2: Ch 3 [counts as first dc], turn; * skip next 2 dc, 5 dc in next dc, skip next 2 dc **, dc in next dc, ch 1, dc in next dc; rep from * across, ending last rep at **, dc in next ch.
Rep Row 2 until rectangle measures approximately 8¾" from beg ch.
Last Row: Ch 1, turn; sc in first dc, * (ch 2, skip next 2 dc, sc in next st) twice **, ch 1, sc in next dc; rep from * across, ending last rep at **; fasten off.

SHELL ST RECTANGLE

(Make 6.)
With A, ch 20.
Row 1 (rs): Dc in 4th ch from hook, * skip next ch, sc in next ch, skip next ch **, 3 dc in next ch; rep from * across, ending last rep at **, 2 dc in last ch.
Note: *Mark last row as rs.*
Row 2: Ch 1, turn; sc in first dc, * skip next dc, 3 dc in next sc, skip next dc, sc in next st; rep from * across.
Row 3: Ch 3, turn; dc in first sc, * skip next dc, sc in next dc, skip next dc **, 3 dc in next sc; rep from * across, ending last rep at **, 2 dc in last sc.
Rep Rows 2 and 3 until rectangle measures approximately 9" from beg ch; fasten off after last row.

HALF-DOUBLE CROCHET RECTANGLE

(Make 6.)
With B, ch 19 loosely.
Row 1 (rs): Hdc in 3rd ch from hook and in ea ch across.
Note: *Mark last row as rs.*
Row 2: Ch 2, turn; hdc in ea hdc across.
Rep Row 2 until rectangle measures approximately 9" from beg ch; fasten off after last row.

TRACK ST RECTANGLE

(Make 6.)
With C, ch 20 loosely.
Row 1 (ws): Sc in 2nd ch from hook and in ea ch across.
Note: *Mark back of last row as rs.*
Row 2: Ch 5, turn; skip first sc, yo 3 times, insert hook in next sc and pull up a lp, (yo and draw through 2 lps on hook) 4 times [dtr made], dtr in next sc and in ea sc across.
Row 3: Ch 1, turn; sc in ea dtr across and in top of tch.
Rows 4 and 5: Ch 1, turn; sc in ea sc across.
Rows 6–15: Rep Rows 2–5 twice, then rep Rows 2 and 3 once more; fasten off after last row. ➔

Project was stitched with Homespun: Baroque #322, Adirondack #319, Regency #320, Tudor #315.

SINGLE CROCHET RECTANGLE
(Make 6.)

With MC, ch 20 loosely.

Row 1 (rs): Sc in 2nd ch from hook and in ea ch across.

Note: Mark last row as rs.

Row 2: Ch 1, turn; sc in bk lp only of ea sc across.

Rep Row 2 until rectangle measures approximately 9" from beg ch; fasten off after last row.

TWIN V-ST RECTANGLE
(Make 6.)

With A, ch 20.

Row 1 (rs): 2 Dc in 5th ch from hook and in next ch, * skip next 2 chs, 2 dc in ea of next 2 chs; rep from * 2 times more, skip next ch, dc in last ch.

Note: Mark last row as rs.

Row 2: Ch 3, turn; skip first 2 dc, * 2 dc in ea of next 2 dc **, skip next 2 dc; rep from * across, ending last rep at **, skip next dc, dc in next ch.

Rep Row 2 until rectangle measures approximately 9" from beg ch; fasten off after last row.

BASIC V-ST RECTANGLE
(Make 6.)

With B, ch 25.

Row 1 (rs): (Dc, ch 2, dc) in 5th ch from hook, * skip next 2 chs, (dc, ch 2, dc) in next ch; rep from * across to last 2 chs, skip next ch, dc in last ch.

Note: Mark last row as rs.

Row 2: Ch 3, turn; (dc, ch 2, dc) in ea ch-2 sp across, skip next dc, dc in next ch.

Rep Row 2 until rectangle measures approximately 9" from beg ch; fasten off after last row.

DOUBLE CROCHET RECTANGLE
(Make 6.)

With C, ch 21 loosely.

Row 1 (rs): Dc in 4th ch from hook and in ea ch across.

Note: Mark last row as rs.

Row 2: Ch 3 [counts as first dc], turn; skip first dc, dc in next dc and in ea dc across, dc in next ch.

Rep Row 2 until rectangle measures approximately 9" from beg ch; fasten off after last row.

ASSEMBLY
Referring to *Assembly Diagram*, whipstitch rectangles tog.

Assembly Diagram

Diagram Key
- Shell Network
- Shell St
- Half-Double Crochet
- Track St
- Single Crochet
- Twin V-St
- Basic V-St
- Double Crochet

Williamsburg Patchwork

This project is ideal for working on the go. Simply crochet the individual rectangles and then whipstitch them together.

MATERIALS

Chunky-weight acrylic yarn, approximately:
36 oz. (1,110 yd.) blue, MC
24 oz. (740 yd.) dark grey, A
12 oz. (370 yd.) tan, B
Sizes J and I crochet hooks or sizes to obtain gauge
Yarn needle

FINISHED SIZE
Approximately 51" x 65"

GAUGE
Ea Rectangle = 7" x 9"

EA RECTANGLE A
(Make 16.)
With larger hook and MC, ch 14.
Foundation (rs): Dc in 6th ch from hook and in next 2 chs, ch 1, skip next ch, dc in next 3 chs, ch 1, skip next ch, dc in last ch.
Note: Mark foundation as rs.
Rnd 1: Ch 3, do not turn; (2 dc, ch 3, 3 dc) around post of last dc made, ch 1, skip next 3 chs, 3 dc in next sp, ch 1, (3 dc, ch 3, 3 dc, ch 3, 3 dc) in next ch-5 sp, (ch 1, skip next 3 dc, 3 dc in next ch-1 sp) twice, ch 3; join with sl st in top of beg ch-3.
Rnd 2: Sl st in next 2 dc and in next ch-3 sp, (ch 3, 2 dc, ch 3, 3 dc) in same ch-3 sp, ch 1, (3 dc in next ch-1 sp, ch 1) twice, (3 dc, ch 3, 3 dc, ch 1) in ea of next 2 ch-3 sps, (3 dc in next ch-1 sp, ch 1) twice, (3 dc, ch 3, 3 dc) in next ch-3 sp, ch 1; join with sl st to top of beg ch-3.
Rnd 3: Sl st in next 2 dc and in next ch-3 sp, (ch 3, 2 dc, ch 3, 3 dc) in same ch-3 sp, * ch 1, (3 dc in next ch-1 sp, ch 1) 3 times, (3 dc, ch 3, 3 dc) in next ch-3 sp, ch 1, 3 dc in next ch-1 sp, ch 1 **, (3 dc, ch 3, 3 dc) in next ch-3 sp; rep from * to ** once; join with sl st to top of beg ch-3.
Rnd 4: Sl st in next 2 dc and in next ch-3 sp, (ch 3, 2 dc, ch 3, 3 dc) in same ch-3 sp, * ch 1, (3 dc in next ch-1 sp, ch 1) 4 times, (3 dc, ch 3, 3 dc) in next ch-3 sp, ch 1, (3 dc in next ch-1 sp, ch 1) twice **, (3 dc, ch 3, 3 dc) in next ch-3 sp; rep from * to ** once; join with sl st to top of beg ch-3.
Rnd 5: Ch 1, sc in same st as joining and in next 2 dc, 5 sc in next ch-3 sp, * sc in ea dc and in ea ch-1 sp across to next ch-3 sp **, 5 sc in next ch-3 sp; rep from * around, ending last rep at **; join with sl st to beg sc; fasten off.

RECTANGLE B
(Make 12.)
Work as for Rectangle A, using A.

RECTANGLE C
(Make 12.)
With larger hook and MC, ch 14.
Foundation (rs): Dc in 6th ch from hook and in next 2 chs, ch 1, skip next ch, dc in next 3 chs, ch 1, skip next ch, dc in last ch; fasten off.
Note: Mark foundation as rs.
Rnd 1: With rs facing and using larger hook, join A with sl st around post of last dc made; (ch 3, 2 dc, ch 3, 3 dc, ch 3, 3 dc) in same sp, ch 1, skip next 3 chs, 3 dc in next ch-1 sp, ch 1, (3 dc, ch 3, 3 dc, ch 3, 3 dc) in next ch-5 sp, ch 1, 3 dc in ➔

No gift shows more thought and love than one that is handmade.

next ch-1 sp, ch 1; join with sl st in top of beg ch-3; fasten off.

Rnd 2: With rs facing, using larger hook, and working across short edge, join MC with sl st in first corner ch-3 sp; (ch 3, 2 dc, ch 3, 3 dc) in same sp as joining, ch 1, (3 dc, ch 3, 3 dc) in next ch-3 sp, ch 1, (3 dc in next ch-1 sp, ch 1) twice, (3 dc, ch 3, 3 dc, ch 1) in ea of next 2 ch-3 sps, (3 dc in next ch-1 sp, ch 1) twice; join with sl st to top of beg ch-3; fasten off.

Rnd 3: With rs facing, using larger hook, join A with sl st in any corner ch-3 sp; (ch 3, 2 dc, ch 3, 3 dc) in same sp as joining, * ch 1, (3 dc in next ch-1 sp, ch 1) across to next ch-3 sp **, (3 dc, ch 3, 3 dc) in next ch-3 sp; rep from * around, ending last rep at **; join with sl st to top of beg ch-3; fasten off.

Rnd 4: With MC, rep Rnd 3; do not fasten off.

Rnd 5: Ch 1, sc in same st as joining and in next 2 dc, 5 sc in next ch-3 sp, * sc in ea dc and in ea ch-1 sp across to next ch-3 sp **, 5 sc in next ch-3 sp; rep from * around, ending last rep at **; join with sl st to beg sc; fasten off.

RECTANGLE D
(Make 9.)
Work as for Rectangle A, using B.

ASSEMBLY
Referring to *Assembly Diagram*,

Assembly Diagram

A	B	A	B	A	B	A
C	D	C	D	C	D	C
A	B	A	B	A	B	A
C	D	C	D	C	D	C
A	B	A	B	A	B	A
C	D	C	D	C	D	C
A	B	A	B	A	B	A

whipstitch rectangles tog.

BORDER
Rnd 1: With rs facing and using smaller hook, join A with sl st in center sc of any corner; (ch 3, dc, ch 1, 2 dc) in same st as joining, * skip next sc, (2 dc in next sc, skip next sc) across to next corner **, (2 dc, ch 1, 2 dc) in corner; rep from * around, ending last rep at **; join with sl st to top of beg ch-3; fasten off.

Rnd 2: With ws facing and using smaller hook, join MC with sl st in any corner ch-1 sp; ch 1, 3 sc in same sp as joining, sc in ea dc around working 3 sc in ea corner ch-1 sp; join with sl st to beg sc; fasten off.

Project was stitched with Homespun: Williamsburg #321, French Provincial #340, Rococo #311.

Chenille Ripple

Nothing is cozier than curling up under a rich chenille throw. The chunky-weight chenille yarn and a large crochet hook let you whip out this comfy afghan in no time.

MATERIALS
Chunky-weight chenille
yarn, approximately:
400 yd. brown, MC
400 yd. tan, A
400 yd. burgundy, B
Size N crochet hook or size
to obtain gauge

FINISHED SIZE
Approximately 46" x 68"

GAUGE
In pat, 13 sts = 7½"; 6 rows = 6"

Note: *To change colors, work last yo of prev st with new color; fasten off old color.*

With MC, ch 79.

Row 1 (ws): Sc in 2nd ch from hook and in next 5 chs, 3 sc in next ch, * sc in next 5 chs, skip next 2 chs, sc in next 5 chs, 3 sc in next ch; rep from * across, sc in last 6 chs: 80 sc.

Row 2 (rs): Ch 3, turn; skip first 2 sc, * dc in next 5 sc, 3 dc in next sc, dc in next 5 sc **, skip next 2 sc; rep from * across, ending last rep at **, skip next sc, dc in last sc.

Row 3: Ch 1, turn; sc in first dc, skip next dc, * sc in next 5 dc, 3 sc in next dc, sc in next 5 dc **, skip next 2 dc; rep from * across, ending last rep at **, skip last dc, sc in top of tch.

Row 4: Ch 3, turn; skip first 2 sc, * dc in next 5 sc, 3 dc in next sc, dc in next 5 sc **, skip next 2 sc; rep from * across, ending last rep at **, skip next sc, dc in last sc.

Rows 5 and 6: Rep Rows 3 and 4 once, changing to A in last st of last row.

Rows 7–12: With A, rep Rows 3 and 4, 3 times, changing to B in last st of last row.

Rows 13–18: With B, rep Rows 3 and 4, 3 times, changing to MC in last st of last row.

Rows 19–22: With MC, rep Rows 3 and 4 twice, changing to A in last st of last row.

Rows 23–26: With A, rep Rows 3 and 4 twice, changing to B in last st of last row.

Rows 27–30: With B, rep Rows 3 and 4 twice, changing to MC in last st of last row.

Rows 31 and 32: With MC, rep Rows 3 and 4 once, changing to A in last st of last row.

Rows 33 and 34: With A, rep Rows 3 and 4 once, changing to B in last st of last row.

Rows 35 and 36: With B, rep Rows 3 and 4 once, changing to MC in last st of last row.

Rows 37–40: With MC, rep Rows 3 and 4 twice, changing to A in last st of last row.

Rows 41–44: With A, rep Rows 3 and 4 twice, changing to B in last st of last row.

Rows 45–48: With B, rep Rows 3 and 4 twice, changing to MC in last st of last row.

Rows 49–54: With MC, rep Rows 3 and 4, 3 times, changing to A in last st of last row.

Rows 55–60: With A, rep Rows 3 and 4, 3 times, changing to B in last st of last row.

Rows 61–66: With B, rep Rows 3 and 4, 3 times; fasten off after last row. ➔

Chenille is soft to the touch as well as appealing to the eye.

Project was stitched with Chenille Thick & Quick: Chocolate #125, Khaki #124, Wine #189.

Dusting of Roses

Let this romantic afghan add a touch of Victorian charm to your bedroom.

MATERIALS

Worsted-weight yarn, approximately:

36 oz. (2,365 yd.) ecru, MC
3 oz. (195 yd.) rose, A
3 oz. (195 yd.) dark rose, B
3 oz. (195 yd.) green, C
Size I crochet hook or size to obtain gauge
Yarn needle

FINISHED SIZE

Approximately 44" x 63"

GAUGE

In pat, Rnds 1–4 = 4½"
Ea Square = 9½" square

PATTERN STITCHES

Back Post Single Crochet (BPsc): Insert hook from back to front around post of st indicated, yo and pull up a lp, yo and draw through both lps on hook.

Picot: Ch 3, sl st in 3rd ch from hook.

SQUARE

(Make 24.)
With MC, ch 4; join with sl st to form a ring.

Rnd 1 (rs): Ch 6, (3 dc, ch 3) 3 times in ring, 2 dc in ring; join with sl st to 3rd ch of beg ch-6.

Note: Mark last rnd as rs.

Rnd 2: Ch 3 [counts as first dc throughout], * (2 dc, ch 3, 2 dc) in next ch-3 sp **, dc in next 3 dc; rep from * around, ending last rep at **, dc in last 2 dc; join with sl st to top of beg ch-3.

Rnds 3–8: Ch 3, dc in ea dc across to next ch-3 sp, * (2 dc, ch 3, 2 dc) in next ch-3 sp **, dc in ea dc across to next ch-3 sp; rep from * around, ending last rep at **, dc in ea dc across; join with sl st to top of beg ch-3.

Rnd 9: Ch 3, 2 dc in same st as joining, skip next 2 dc, (3 dc in next dc, skip next 3 dc) 3 times, * (3 dc, ch 3, 3 dc) in next ch-3 sp, (skip next 3 dc, 3 dc in next dc) twice **, (skip next 2 dc, 3 dc in next dc) 4 times, skip next 3 dc, (3 dc in next dc, skip next 3 dc) twice; rep from * around, ending last rep at **, skip next 2 dc, (3 dc in next dc, skip next 2 dc) twice; join with sl st to top of beg ch-3; fasten off.

ASSEMBLY

Afghan is 6 squares long by 4 squares wide. Whipstitch squares tog.

BORDER

Rnd 1 (rs): With rs facing and working across short edge, join MC with slip st in first corner ch-3 sp; ch 1, 3 sc in same sp as joining, * work 123 sc evenly sp across to next corner ch-3 sp, 3 sc in corner ch-3 sp, work 183 sc evenly sp across to next corner ch-3 sp **, 3 sc in corner ch-3 sp; rep from * to ** once; join with sl st to beg sc.

Rnd 2: Ch 1, 2 sc in same st as joining, * 3 sc in next sc, 2 sc in next sc **, sc in ea sc across to next corner 3-sc group, 2 sc in next sc; rep from * around, ending last rep at **, sc in ea sc across; join with sl st to beg sc.

Rnd 3: Sl st in next 3 sc, (ch 3, 2 dc, ch 3, 3 dc) in same st as last sl st made, ch 3, * skip next 3 sc, (dc in next 3 sc, ch 3, skip next 3 sc) across to center sc of next corner 3-sc group **, (3 dc, ch 3) twice in corner sc; rep from * around, ending last rep at **; join with sl st to 3rd ch of beg ch-3.

Rnd 4: Sl st in next dc, ch 6, * dc in next ch-3 sp, ch 3, skip next dc **, dc in next dc, ch 3; rep from * around, ending last rep at **; join with sl st to top of beg ch-6.

Rnd 5: Ch 3, [(dc, ch 3, dc) in next ch-3 sp, dc in next dc] 3 times, * (dc in next ch-3 sp, ch 3, skip next dc, dc in next ch-3 sp and in next dc) across to within 2 ch-3 sps of next corner dc, [(dc, ch 3, dc) in next ch-3 sp, dc in next dc] 4 times; rep from * 2 times more, (dc in next ch-3 sp, ch 3, skip next dc, dc in next ch-3 sp and in next dc) across to last ch-3 sp, (dc, ch 3, dc) in last ch-3 sp; join with sl st to top of beg ch-3.

Rnd 6: Ch 6, * dc in next ch-3 sp, ch 3, skip next dc **, dc in next dc, ch 3; rep from * around, ending last rep at **; join with sl st to 3rd ch of beg ch-6.

Rnd 7: Ch 1, sc in same st as joining, * ch 7, (sl st, ch 4, sl st) in 4th ch from hook, ch 3, skip next dc **, sc in next dc; rep from * around, ending last rep at **; join with sl st to beg sc; fasten off.

FINISHING

Large Flower (Make 5.)
With A, ch 8; join with sl st to form a ring.

Rnd 1 (rs): Ch 1, 18 sc in ring; join with sl st to beg sc.

Rnd 2: Ch 6, skip next 2 sc,

Project was stitched with Wool-Ease: Fisherman #099, Rose Heather #140, Dark Rose Heather #139, Green Heather #130.

* hdc in next sc, ch 4, skip next 2 sc; rep from * around; join with sl st to 2nd ch of beg ch-6.

Rnd 3: Ch 1, (sc, hdc, 3 dc, hdc, sc) in ea ch-4 sp around; join with sl st to beg sc.

Rnd 4: Ch 1, working behind petals, BPsc around first st on Rnd 2, ch 5, * BPsc around next hdc on Rnd 2, ch 5; rep from * around; join with sl st to first BPsc.

Rnd 5: Ch 1, (sc, hdc, 5 dc, hdc, sc) in ea ch-5 sp around; join with sl st to beg sc.

Rnd 6: Ch 1, working behind petals, BPsc around first BPsc on Rnd 4, ch 6, * BPsc around next BPsc on Rnd 4, ch 6; rep from * around; join with sl st to first BPsc.

Rnd 7: Ch 1, (sc, hdc, 7 dc, hdc, sc) in ea ch-6 sp around; join with sl st to beg sc.

Rnd 8: Ch 3, working behind petals, * sl st in back 2 legs of center dc of next petal, ch 6; rep from * around, skip beg ch-3; join with sl st to first sl st.

Rnd 9: Ch 1, (sc, hdc, dc, 5 tr, dc, hdc, sc) in ea ch-6 sp around; join with sl st to beg sc.

Rnd 10: * Ch 3, skip next 2 sts, sc in next tr, work picot, (ch 1, skip next tr, sc in next tr, work picot) twice, ch 3, skip next 3 sts **, sl st in next sc; rep from * around, ending last rep at **; join with sl st in same st as joining on Rnd 9; fasten off.

Small Flower (Make 16.)
Note: *Make 8 using A and 8 using B.*
With color indicated, work same

as Large Flower through Rnd 5; fasten off after last rnd.

Leaf 1 (Make 11.)
With C, ch 15 loosely.
Rnd 1 (rs): Sc in 2nd ch from hook, * hdc in next ch, dc in next 3 chs, tr in next 4 chs, dc in next 3 chs, hdc in next ch **, (sc, ch 3, sc) in last ch, working in free loop of beg ch; rep from * to ** once, sc in next ch, ch 3; do not join.
Rnd 2: Sc in first 2 sts, work picot, (sc in next 2 sts, work picot) 6 times, sl st in next ch-3 sp, work picot, sl st in next sc and in ea st across to next ch-3 sp, sl st in ch-3 sp; fasten off.

Leaf 2 (Make 11.)
With C, ch 15 loosely. →

Rnd 1 (rs): Sc in 2nd ch from hook, * hdc in next ch, dc in next 3 chs, tr in next 4 chs, dc in next 3 chs, hdc in next ch **, (sc, ch 3, sc) in last ch, working in free loop of beg ch, rep from * to ** once, sc in next ch, ch 3; join with sl st in beg sc.

Rnd 2: Sl st in ea st across to next ch-3 sp, (sc, ch 4, sl st in 3rd ch from hook, ch 1, sc) in ch-3 sp, (work picot, sc in next 2 sts) across to next ch-3 sp, sl st in ch-3 sp; fasten off.

Using *Placement Diagram* as a guide, sew flowers and leaves to afghan.

Placement Diagram

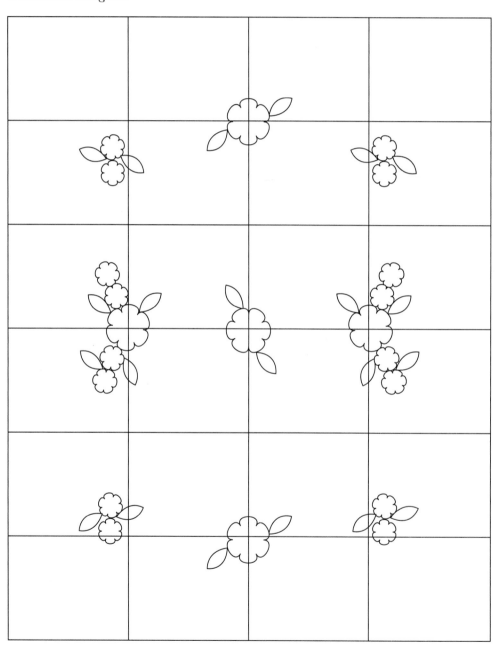

Ebony & Ivory

The stark contrast of black and white in this afghan looks spectacular with a contemporary home decor.

FINISHED SIZE
Approximately 41" x 64"

GAUGE
In patt with largest hook,
14 sc = 5"
Ea Strip = 4½" x 64"

Note: *To change colors, work last
yo of prev st with new color.*

PATTERN STITCH
Long dc (Ldc): Yo, insert hook
in st indicated, pull up lp even
with last row made, (yo and draw
through 2 lps) twice.

STRIP 1
(Make 6.)
With MC and largest hook, ch
170 loosely.
Row 1 (rs): Sc in 2nd ch from
hook and in ea ch across: 169 sc.
Note: *Mark last st made as rs and
bottom edge.*
Row 2: Ch 1, turn; sc in ea sc
across, change to CC.
Rows 3 and 4: Ch 1, turn; sc in
ea sc across; at end of last row
change to MC.
Row 5: Ch 1, turn; sc in first sc,
* Ldc in sc 2 rows below next sc,

sc in next sc; rep from * across.
Row 6: Ch 1, turn; sc in ea st
across, change to CC.
Note: *Beg working in rnds.*
Rnd 1 (rs): Ch 3, turn; dc in
first sc, (skip next sc, 2 dc in
next sc) across, ch 1, 2 dc in end
of Row 5, 3 dc in end of ea of
next 2 rows, 2 dc in end of next
row, ch 1, skip next row, 2 dc in
free lp of next ch, (skip next ch,
2 dc in free lp of next ch) across,
ch 1, 2 dc in end of Row 2, 3 dc
in end of ea of next 2 rows, 2 dc
in next row, ch 1; join with sl st
to top of beg ch-3; fasten off.
Rnd 2: With rs facing and
largest hook, join MC with sl st
in last ch-1 sp made; (ch 3, dc,
ch 1, 2 dc) in same sp as joining,
* skip next 2 sts, (2 dc in sp
before next dc, skip next 2 dc)
across to next ch-1 sp, (2 dc,
ch 1, 2 dc) in next ch-1 sp, skip
next 2 dc, (2 dc in sp before
next dc, skip next 2 dc) 4 times
**, (2 dc, ch 1, 2 dc) in next
ch-1 sp; rep from * to ** once;
join with sl st to top of beg ch-3;
fasten off.

STRIP 2
(Make 5.)
Work as for Strip 1, reversing
MC and CC.

ASSEMBLY
Join Strips together, alternating
colors as folls: with rs and bottom edges tog, working in bk lps
only, and using largest hook, join
MC with sl st in first dc after
corner ch-1; sl st in ea dc across

to next corner ch-1; fasten off.
Rep for remaining Strips.

BORDER
Rnd 1: With rs facing and medium hook, join MC with sl st in
any dc; ch 1, sc in same st as
joining and in ea dc around
working 3 sc in ea corner ch-1
sp; join with sl st to beg sc;
change to smallest hook.
Rnd 2: Ch 1, working from left
to right, sc in same st and in ea
sc around [reverse sc]; join with
sl st to beg sc; fasten off.

This afghan

makes a lovely

anniversary gift.

Give it along

with a bottle

of champagne for

a cozy, romantic

celebration.

Project was stitched with Wool-Ease: Black Frost #502, White Frost #501.

Fringe Benefits

This afghan's outer fringe is mirrored in the fringed inner rectangle.
The variegated yarn gives both added depth of color.

MATERIALS
Sport-weight wool blend
yarn, approximately:
40 oz. (3,480 yd.) variegated
Size K crochet hook or size
to obtain gauge

FINISHED SIZE
Approximately 40" x 55", not
including fringe

GAUGE
In pat, 11 dc and 5½ rows = 4"

Note: *Afghan is stitched holding
2 strands of yarn tog throughout.
Because of the different number of
tones and the length of each color,
make sure you start both skeins
with the same color pat.*

Ch 111.
Row 1 (rs): Dc in 4th ch from
hook and in ea ch across: 109 sts.
Row 2: Ch 3, turn; skip first dc,
dc in next dc and in ea dc across,
dc in top of beg ch.
Rows 3–14: Ch 3, turn; skip
first dc, dc in next dc and in ea
dc across, dc in top of tch.
Rows 15 and 16: Ch 3, turn;
skip first dc, dc in next 26 dc,
place marker around last dc
made for Fringe placement, dc in
next 56 dc, place marker around

last dc made for Fringe placement, dc in next 25 dc and in
top of tch.
Rows 17–59: Ch 3, turn; skip
first dc, dc in next dc and in
each dc across, dc in top of tch.
Rows 60 and 61: Rep Rows 15
and 16.
Rows 62–76: Ch 3, turn; skip
first dc, dc in next dc and in
each dc across, dc in top of tch;
fasten off after last row.

FINISHING
For fringe, referring to page 143
of General Directions, cut
3 (5") lengths of yarn for each
yarn section. Knot yarn section
around post of ea dc indicated.

Horizontal Fringe
Knot 1 yarn section around post
of ea st on first 3 rows and last
3 rows of Afghan. Knot 1 yarn
section around post of ea dc,
beginning around first marked dc
and ending around last marked
dc on Rows 15, 16, 60, and 61.

Vertical Fringe
Knot 1 yarn section around post
of first 3 sts and last 3 sts of ea
row across length of Afghan.
Knot 1 yarn section around post
of 27th, 28th, 29th, 80th, 81st,
and 82nd st of ea row between
markers to form inner square of
fringe.

Project was stitched with Wool-Ease Sportweight: Autumn Print #233.

Patriotic Picnic Blanket

This star-spangled blanket measures almost four feet by five feet, so there's plenty of room for my family and all of our Fourth of July picnic fare. And because it is made from 100%-cotton yarn, it is an ideal summer-weight pallet or throw.

MATERIALS

100% worsted-weight cotton yarn, approximately:
25 oz. (1,180 yd.) white, MC
20 oz. (945 yd.) red, A
20 oz. (945 yd.) blue, B
Size H crochet hook or size to obtain gauge

FINISHED SIZE

Approximately 46" x 62"

GAUGE

In pat, 7 sc and 8 rows = 2"

Note: *To change colors, work last yo of prev st with new color, dropping prev color to ws of work.*

Each Square on the Chart represents one single crochet stitch. Because the work is turned after each row, be sure to read all right side rows from right to left and all wrong side rows from left to right.

With A, ch 29, drop A, pick up MC, yo and pull through lp on hook [color change ch made], ch 34, drop MC, pick up A, yo and pull through lp on hook, ch 34, drop A, pick up MC, yo and pull through lp on hook, ch 37: 137 chs.

Row 1 (rs): Sc in 2nd ch from hook and in next 35 chs, change to A, sc in next 35 chs, change to MC, sc in next 35 chs, change to A, sc in last 30 chs: 136 sc.

Note: *Mark last row as rs.*

Row 2 (ws): Ch 1, turn; reading *Chart* on pages 26 and 27 from left to right, sc in first 31 sc, change to MC, sc in next 34 sc, change to A, sc in next 35 sc, change to MC, sc in last 36 sc.

Row 3: Ch 1, turn; reading *Chart* from right to left, sc in first 36 sc, change to A, sc in next 35 sc, change to MC, sc in next 34 sc, change to A, sc in last 31 sc.

Rows 4–220: Cont foll *Chart* as est, reading even (ws) rows from left to right and odd (rs) rows from right to left; fasten off after last row.

BORDER

Rnd 1: With rs facing, join A with sl st in any corner; ch 1, 3 sc in same st as joining, sc evenly around working 3 sc in ea corner; join with sl st to beg sc.

Rnds 2–4: Ch 1, do not turn; sc in same st as joining and in ea sc around working 3 sc in ea corner sc; join with sl st to beg sc; fasten off after last rnd.

Rnd 5: With rs facing, join MC with sl st in any sc; ch 1, sc in same st as joining and in ea sc around working 3 sc in ea corner sc; join with sl st to beg sc.

Rnds 6–9: Ch 1, do not turn; sc in same st as joining and in ea sc around working 3 sc in ea corner sc; join with sl st to beg sc; fasten off after last rnd.

Rnd 10: With rs facing, join B with sl st in any sc; ch 1, sc in same st as joining and in ea sc around working 3 sc in each corner sc; join with sl st to beg sc.

Rnds 11–13: Ch 1, do not turn; sc in same st as joining and in ea sc around working 3 sc in ea corner sc; join with sl st to beg sc; fasten off after last rnd. →

Project was stitched with Kitchen Cotton: White #100, Poppy Red #112, Navy #110.

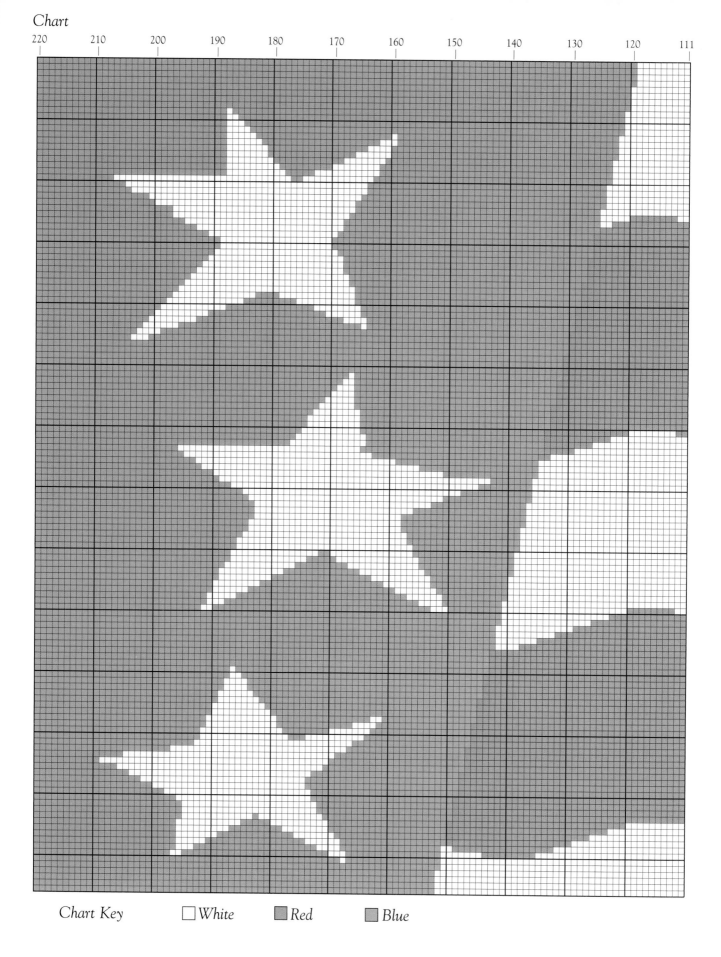

Chart Key ☐ White ▨ Red ▨ Blue

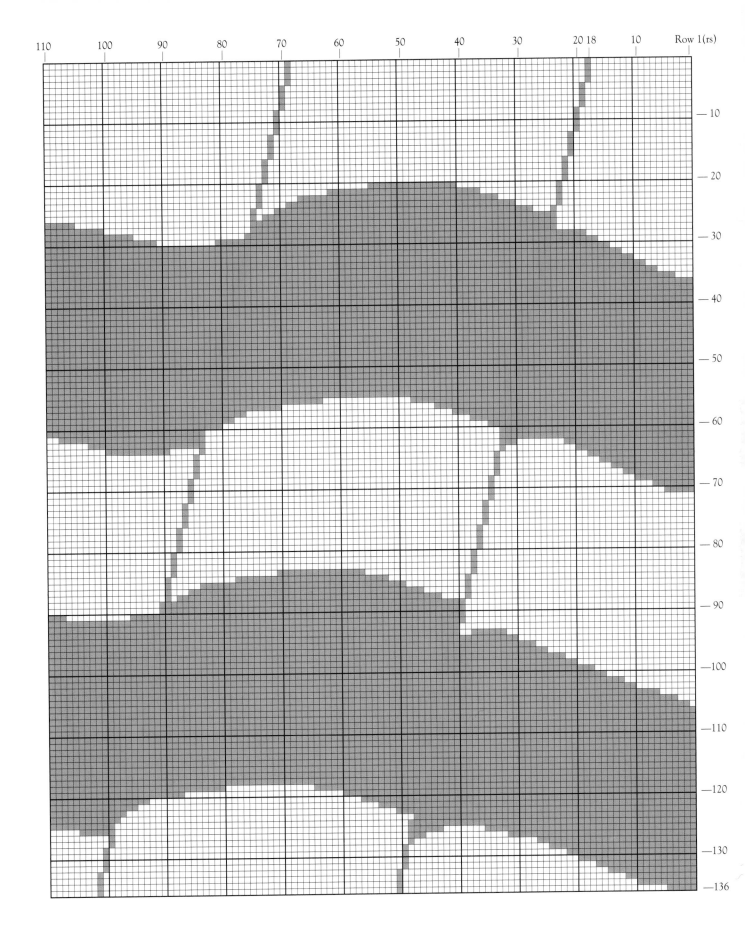

Powdery Waves

Update a classic ripple design with a contemporary yarn. The thick-and-thin texture of the yarn gives this afghan a soft feel and a unique look.

MATERIALS

Thick-and-thin textured
yarn, approximately:
500 yd. mauve, MC
500 yd. grey, A
400 yd. green, B
Size N crochet hook or size
to obtain gauge

FINISHED SIZE

Approximately 40" x 60"

GAUGE

In pat, 9 sts = 4"; 4 rows = 3½ "

Note: *To change colors, work last yo of prev st with new color; fasten off old color.*

PATTERN STITCH

Dec: (Yo, insert hook in next st, yo and pull up a lp, yo and pull through 2 lps) 3 times, yo and pull through all 4 lps on hook.

With MC, ch 93.
Row 1 (rs): Dc in 3rd ch from hook and in next 3 chs, dec, dc in next 3 chs, * 3 dc in next ch, dc in next 3 chs, dec, dc in next 3 chs; rep from * across, 2 dc in last ch: 91 sts.
Row 2: Ch 3 [counts as first dc throughout], turn; dc in first 4 dc, * dec, dc in next 3 dc **, 3 dc in next dc, dc in next 3 dc; rep from * across, ending last rep at **, 2 dc in top of beg ch, change to A.
Rows 3–6: Ch 3, turn; dc in first 4 dc, * dec, dc in next 3 dc **, 3 dc in next dc, dc in next 3 dc; rep from * across, ending last rep at **, 2 dc in last dc, changing to MC in last dc of last row.

Rows 7 and 8: Ch 3, turn; dc in first 4 dc, * dec, dc in next 3 dc **, 3 dc in next dc, dc in next 3 dc; rep from * across, ending last rep at **, 2 dc in last dc, changing to B in last dc of last row.
Rows 9–14: Rep Rows 3–8, changing to A in last dc of last row.
Rows 15–68: Rep Rows 3–14, 4 times, then rep Rows 3–8 once; fasten off after last row.

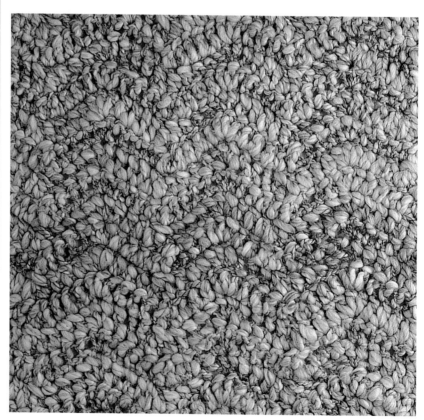

Project was stitched with Woolspun: Dusty Mauve #141, Slate Grey #149, Sage #123.

Mother's Day Memories

Breakfast in bed with Nikko and Giovanna is a cozy affair when we're snuggled under this extrasoft, lightweight coverlet.

MATERIALS
Sport-weight yarn, approximately:
30 oz. (2,015 yd.) lilac
Size H crochet hook or size to obtain gauge
Yarn needle

FINISHED SIZE
Approximately 45" x 55"

GAUGE
Ea Square = 10"

PATTERN STITCHES
Beg cl: Ch 4, * yo twice, insert hook in next tr, yo and pull up lp, (yo and draw through 2 lps) twice; rep from * 3 times more, yo and draw through all 5 lps on hook.
Cl: * Yo twice, insert hook in next tr, yo and pull up lp, (yo and draw through 2 lps) twice; rep from * 4 times more, yo and draw through all 6 lps on hook.
Picot: Ch 4, sl st in 4th ch from hook.

SQUARE
(Make 20.)
Ch 8, join with sl st to form a ring.
Rnd 1 (rs): Ch 3 [counts as first dc throughout], 23 dc in ring; join with sl st to top of beg ch-3: 24 dc.
Note: Mark last rnd as rs.
Rnd 2: Ch 6, dc in same st as joining, ch 3, skip next 2 dc, dc in next dc, ch 3, skip next 2 dc, * (dc, ch 3) twice in next dc, skip next 2 dc, dc in next dc, ch 3; rep from * around; join with sl st to 3rd ch of beg ch-6.
Rnd 3: Slip st in first ch-3 sp, ch 4, (4 tr, ch 3, 5 tr) in same ch-3 sp, * ch 2, skip next ch-3 sp, (tr, ch 3, tr) in next dc, ch 2, skip next ch-3 sp **, (5 tr, ch 3, 5 tr) in next ch-3 sp; rep from * around, ending last rep at **; join with sl st to top of beg ch-4.
Rnd 4: Beg cl over next 4 tr, ch 3, * (5 tr, ch 3) twice in next ch-3 sp, cl over next 5 tr, ch 3, skip next ch-2 sp, (tr, ch 3) twice

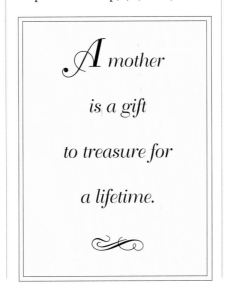

A mother is a gift to treasure for a lifetime.

in next ch-3 sp, skip next ch-2 sp **, cl over next 5 tr, ch 3; rep from * around, ending last rep at **; join with sl st to top of beg cl.
Rnd 5: Sl st in next 3 chs and in next tr, beg cl over next 4 tr, ch 3, * (5 tr, ch 3) twice in next ch-3 sp, cl over next 5 tr, ch 3, skip next 2 ch-3 sps, (tr, ch 3) 4 times in next ch-3 sp, skip next 2 ch-3 sps **, cl over next 5 tr, ch 3; rep from * around, ending last rep at **; join with sl st to top of beg cl.
Rnd 6: Sl st in next 3 chs and in next tr, beg cl over next 4 tr, ch 3, * (5 tr, ch 3) twice in next ch-3 sp, cl over next 5 tr, ch 3, skip next 2 ch-3 sps, (tr, ch 3) twice in ea of next 3 ch-3 sps, skip next 2 ch-3 sps **, cl over next 5 tr, ch 3; rep from * around, ending last rep at **; join with sl st to top of beg cl.
Rnd 7: Sl st in next 3 chs and in next tr, beg cl over next 4 tr, ch 3, * (5 tr, ch 3) twice in next ch-3 sp, cl over next 5 tr, ch 3, skip next 2 ch-3 sps, (tr, ch 1) twice in next ch-3 sp, (dc, ch 1) twice in ea of next 3 ch-3 sps, (tr, ch 1, tr) in next ch-3 sp, ch 3, skip next 2 ch-3 sps **, cl over next 5 tr, ch 3; rep from * around, ending last rep at **; →

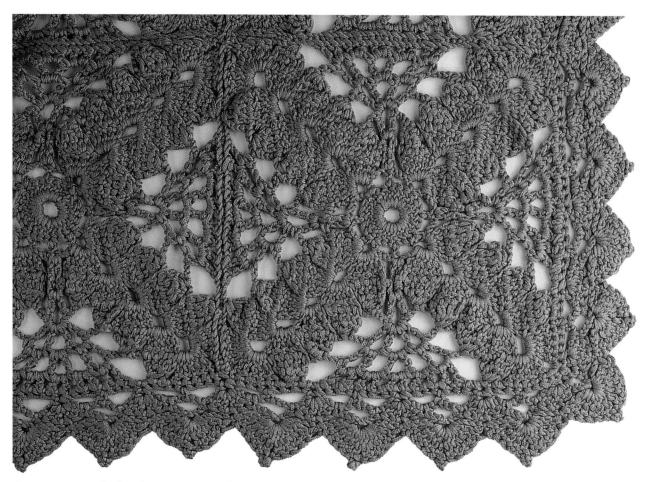

Project was stitched with Microspun: Lilac #144.

join with sl st to top of beg cl; fasten off.

ASSEMBLY
Afghan is 5 squares long and 4 squares wide. Whipstitch squares tog.

BORDER
Rnd 1 (rs): With rs facing and working across short edge, join yarn with sl st in first corner ch-3 sp; ch 1, 3 sc in same ch-3 sp, * work 127 sc evenly spaced across to next corner ch-3 sp, 3 sc in corner ch-3 sp, work 159 sc evenly spaced across to next corner ch-3 sp **, 3 sc in corner ch-3 sp; rep from * to ** once; join with sl st to beg sc.

Rnd 2: Ch 1, sc in same st as joining, (ch 3, sc in next sc) twice, * (ch 5, skip next 3 sc, sc in next sc) across to center sc of next corner, (ch 3, sc in next sc) twice; rep from * 2 times more, ch 5, skip next 3 sc, (sc in next sc, ch 5, skip next 3 sc) across; join with sl st to beg sc.

Rnd 3: Ch 3, 3 dc in same st as joining, sc in next ch-3 sp, ch 5, sc in next ch-3 sp, * 4 dc in next sc, sc in next sp, ch 5, sc in next sp; rep from * around; join with sl st to top of beg ch-3.

Rnd 4: Sl st in next dc, ch 1, * sc in sp before next dc, ch 4, sc in next ch-5 sp, ch 4, skip next sc and next 2 dc; rep from * around; join with sl st to beg sc.

Rnd 5: Ch 1, sc in same st as joining, * (5 tr, picot, 5 tr) in next sc **, sc in next sc; rep from * around, ending last rep at **; join with sl st to beg sc; fasten off.

LeMoyne Star

Based on a time-honored quilt pattern, this throw combines the softness of an afghan and the interesting pattern of a quilt.

MATERIALS
Chunky yarn, pproximately:
10 oz. (930 yd.) off-white, MC
18 oz. (560 yd.) rose, A
12 oz. (370 yd.) variegated, B
12 oz. (370 yd.) blue, C
12 oz. (370 yd.) green, D
Size K crochet hook or size to obtain gauge
Yarn needle

FINISHED SIZE
Approximately 70" square

GAUGE
In pat, 5 sc = 2"; 5 rows = 1¾"

Note: To change colors, work last yo of prev st with new color; dropping unused color to ws.

SMALL SQUARES
(4" x 4")
Solid (Make 4.)
With MC, ch 11 loosely.
Row 1 (rs): Sc in 2nd ch from hook and in ea ch across.
Rows 2–11: Ch 1, turn; sc in ea sc across; fasten off after last row.

Two-tone (Make 20.)
With A, ch 11 loosely.
Row 1 (rs): Sc in 2nd ch from hook and in ea ch across, change to MC.
Row 2: Ch 1, turn; sc in first sc, change to A, sc in last 9 sc.
Rows 3–11: Cont foll *Chart 1*, page 35, as est, reading odd (rs) rows from right to left and even (ws) rows from left to right; fasten off after last row.

MEDIUM SQUARES
(5" x 5")
Solid (Make 4.)
With MC, ch 14 loosely.
Row 1 (rs): Sc in 2nd ch from hook and in ea ch across.
Rows 2–14: Ch 1, turn; sc in ea sc across; fasten off after last row.

Two-tone A (Make 4.)
With A, ch 14 loosely.
Row 1 (rs): Sc in 2nd ch from hook and in ea ch across, change to MC.
Row 2: Ch 1, turn; sc in first sc, change to A, sc in last 12 sc.
Rows 3–14: Cont foll *Chart 2*, page 35, as est, reading odd (rs) rows from right to left and even (ws) rows from left to right; fasten off after last row.

Two-tone B (Make 4.)
With B, ch 14 loosely.
Row 1 (rs): Sc in 2nd ch from hook and in ea ch across, change to A.
Row 2: Ch 1, turn; sc in first sc, change to B, sc in last 12 sc.
Rows 3–14: Cont foll *Chart 3*, page 35, as est, reading odd (rs) rows from right to left and even (ws) rows from left to right; fasten off after last row.

Two-tone C (Make 4.)
With B, ch 14 loosely.
Row 1 (rs): Sc in 2nd ch from hook and in ea ch across.
Row 2: Ch 1, turn; sc in first 12 sc, change to MC, sc in last sc.
Row 3: Ch 1, turn; sc in first 2 sc, change to B, sc in last 11 sc.
Rows 4–14: Cont foll *Chart 4*, page 35, as est, reading even (ws) rows from left to right and odd (rs) rows from right to left; fasten off after last row.

LARGE SQUARES
(7" x 7")
Solid (Make 4.)
With MC, ch 18 loosely.
Row 1 (rs): Sc in 2nd ch from hook and in ea ch across. ➔

Rows 2–18: Ch 1, turn; sc in ea sc across; fasten off after last row.

Two-tone (Make 24.)
Note: Make the number of squares specified following Chart 5 *and substituting CC as indicated: MC & A, 6; MC & B, 6; MC & C, 4; MC & D, 4.*

With A, ch 18 loosely.
Row 1 (rs): Sc in 2nd ch from hook and in ea ch across, change to MC.
Row 2: Ch 1, turn; sc in first sc, change to A, sc in last 16 sc.
Rows 3–18: Cont foll *Chart 5* as est, reading odd (rs) rows from right to left and even (ws) rows from left to right; fasten off after last row.

Chart 1 (4" x 4")

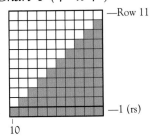

Chart 2 (5" x 5")

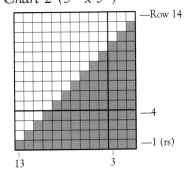

Chart 3 (5" x 5")

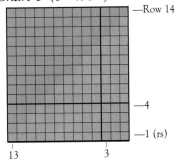

Chart 4 (5" x 5")

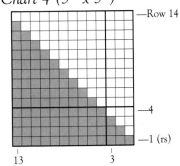

Chart 5 (7" x 7")

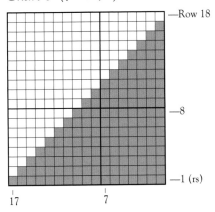

Each Square on the charts represents one single crochet stitch. Because the work is turned after each row, be sure to read all right side rows from right to left and all wrong side rows from left to right.

Chart Key
☐ Off-white, MC ▦ Blue, C
▨ Rose, A ▦ Green, D
▨ Variegated, B →

Assembly Diagram

ASSEMBLY

Following *Assembly Diagram* (see page 35), whipstitch Medium Squares and Small Squares tog as indicated to form inner square.

INSIDE BORDER

Rnd 1: With rs facing, join C with sl st in any corner; ch 1, * 3 sc in corner, sc evenly across to next corner; rep from * around; join with sl st to beg sc.

Rnds 2 and 3: Ch 1, sc in same st as joining and in ea sc around working 3 sc in center sc of ea corner; join with sl st to beg sc; fasten off after last rnd.

Rnd 4: With rs facing, join B with sl st in any sc; ch 1, sc in same st as joining and in each sc around working 3 sc in ea corner sc; join with sl st to beg sc.

Rnds 5 and 6: Ch 1, sc in same st as joining and in ea sc around working 3 sc in center sc of ea corner; join with sl st to beg sc; fasten off after last rnd.

Rnd 7: With rs facing, join B with sl st in any sc; ch 1, sc in same st as joining and in each sc around working 3 sc in ea corner sc; join with sl st to beg sc.

Rnds 8 and 9: Ch 1, sc in same st as joining and in ea sc around working 3 sc in center sc of ea corner; join with sl st to beg sc; fasten off after last rnd.

LARGE SQUARE ASSEMBLY

Following *Assembly Diagram* (see page 35), whipstitch Large Squares tog and then sew squares to afghan center.

Project was stitched with Homespun: Deco #309, Antique #307, Mission #303, Colonial #302, Country #304.

OUTSIDE BORDER

Rnd 1: With rs facing, join C with sl st in any corner; ch 1, * 3 sc in corner, sc evenly across to next corner; rep from * around; join with sl st to beg sc.

Rnds 2 and 3: Ch 1, sc in same st as joining and in ea sc around working 3 sc in center sc of ea corner; join with sl st to beg sc; fasten off after last rnd.

Rnd 4: With rs facing, join MC with sl st in any sc; ch 1, sc in same st as joining and in ea sc around working 3 sc in center sc of ea corner; join with sl st to beg sc.

Rnd 5: Ch 1, sc in same st as joining and in ea sc around working 3 sc in ea corner sc; join with sl st to beg sc; fasten off.

Rnd 6: With rs facing, join B with sl st in any sc; ch 1, sc in same st as joining and in ea sc around working 3 sc in center sc of ea corner; join with sl st to beg sc.

Rnds 7–10: Rep Rnds 2–5.

Rnd 11: With D, rep Rnd 6.

Rnds 12–14: Ch 1, sc in same st as joining and in ea sc around working 3 sc in ea corner sc; join with sl st to beg sc; fasten off after last rnd.

Rnds 15 and 16: Rep Rnds 4 and 5.

Rnds 17–20: With A, rep Rnds 11–14.

Diamonds Are a Girl's Best Friend

Alternating ivory and taupe diamonds creates an interesting design on this afghan. The 14"-square pillow continues the motif with an ivory diamond on one side and a taupe diamond on the opposite side.

AFGHAN

MATERIALS
Chunky-weight acrylic
    yarn, approximately:
24 oz. (740 yd.) brown, MC
24 oz. (740 yd.) tan, CC
Size K crochet hook or size
    to obtain gauge
Yarn needle

FINISHED SIZE
Approximately 46" x 55"

GAUGE
In pat, 5 sc and 5 rows = 2"

Note: *To change colors, work last yo of prev st with new color, dropping prev color to ws of work.*

PATTERN STITCH
Long sc (Lsc): Working around previous rnd(s), insert hook in st indicated, pull up a lp even with lp on hook, yo and draw through both lps on hook.

SQUARE 1
(Make 12.)
With MC, ch 26.
Row 1 (rs): Sc in 2nd ch from hook and in next 11 chs, change to CC, sc in next sc, change to MC, sc in last 12 chs.
Row 2 (ws): Ch 1, turn; sc in first 11 sc, change to CC, sc in next 3 sc, change to MC, sc in last 11 sc.
Rows 3–26: Cont foll *Chart* as est, reading odd (rs) rows from right to left and even (ws) rows

from left to right; fasten off after last row.

SQUARE 2
(Make 8.)
Work as for Square 1, reversing MC and CC.

ASSEMBLY
Referring to *Assembly Diagram* (see page 39), whipstitch squares tog.

TRIM
First Side: With rs facing and working across long edge, join MC with sl st in first corner; ch 1, work 133 sc evenly spaced across end of rows to next corner, changing color as needed to match squares; fasten off.
Second Side: Work same as first side.

BORDER
Rnd 1: With rs facing and working across short edge, join CC with sl st in end of trim on first corner; ch 1, * work 95 sc evenly spaced across to next corner, 3 sc in first sc on trim, sc in ea sc across to last sc on trim, 3 sc in next sc; repeat from * once; join with sl st to beg sc; fasten off: 464 sc.
Rnd 2: With rs facing, join MC with sl st in any sc; ch 1, sc in same st as joining and in ea sc around working 3 sc in center sc of each corner; join with sl st to beg sc.
Rnds 3–5: Ch 1, sc in same st as joining and in ea sc around working 3 sc in center sc of ea corner; join with sl st to beg sc; fasten off after last rnd.

Chart

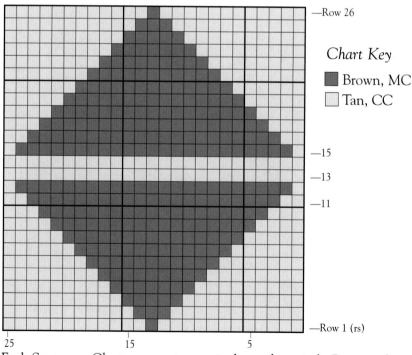

—Row 26

Chart Key
■ Brown, MC
□ Tan, CC

—15
—13
—11

—Row 1 (rs)

25   15   5

Each Square on *Chart* represents one single crochet stitch. Because the work is turned after each row, be sure to read all right side rows from right to left and all wrong side rows from left to right.

Rnd 6: With rs facing, join CC with sl st in center sc of any corner; ch 1, 3 sc in same st as joining, * sc in next 2 sc, Lsc in sc 1 rnd below next sc, Lsc in sc 2 rnds below next sc, Lsc in sc 3 rnds below next sc, Lsc in sc 2 rnds below next sc, Lsc in sc 1 rnd below next sc, (sc in next 7 sc, Lsc in sc 1 rnd below next sc, Lsc in sc 2 rnds below next sc, Lsc in sc 3 rnds below next sc, Lsc in sc 2 rnds below next sc, Lsc in sc 1 rnd below next sc) across to within 2 sc of next corner sc, sc in next 2 sc **, 3 sc in corner sc; rep from * around, ending last rep at **; join with sl st to beg sc.

Rnd 7: Ch 1, sc in same st as joining and in ea st around working 3 sc in each corner sc; join with sl st to beg sc; fasten off.

Assembly Diagram

*Afghan and pillow were
stitched with Homespun:
Deco #309, Rococo #311.*

*Stitch the diamond
afghan for a special
occasion; then continue
the theme by making
matching pillows for the
next gift-giving event.*

REVERSIBLE PILLOW

MATERIALS

Chunky-weight yarn, approximately:
6 oz. (185 yd.) brown, MC
6 oz. (185 yd.) tan, CC
12"-square pillow form
Size K crochet hook or size to obtain gauge
Yarn needle

FINISHED SIZE
Approximately 14" square

GAUGE
In pat, 5 sc and 5 rows = 2"

Note: *To change colors, work last yo of prev st with new color, dropping prev color to ws of work.*

PATTERN STITCH

Long sc (Lsc): Working around previous rnd(s), insert hook in st indicated, pull up a lp even with lp on hook, yo and draw through both lps on hook.

SQUARE 1
(Make 1.)
With CC, ch 32 loosely.
Row 1 (ws): Sc in 2nd ch from hook and in ea ch across.
Note: *Mark back of last row as rs.*
Rows 2–4: Ch 1, turn; sc in ea sc across.
Row 5: Ch 1, turn; sc in first 15 sc, change to MC, sc in next sc, change to CC, sc in last 15 sc.
Rows 6–34: Ch 1, turn; cont foll *Chart* as est, reading even (rs) rows from right to left and odd (ws) rows from left to right; fasten off after last row.

SQUARE 2
(Make 1.)
Work as for Square 1, reversing CC and MC.

ASSEMBLY
Holding squares with ws tog, sew tog inserting pillow form before closing.

BORDER
Rnd 1 (rs): Join MC with sl st in any corner; ch 1, * 3 sc in corner, work 29 sc evenly spaced across to next corner; repeat from * around; join with sl st to beg sc; fasten off: 128 sc.
Rnd 2: With rs facing, join CC with sl st in any sc; ch 1, sc in same st as joining and in ea sc around working 3 sc in center sc of each corner; join with sl st to beg sc.
Rnds 3–5: Ch 1, sc in same st as joining and in ea sc around working 3 sc in center sc of ea corner; join with sl st to beg sc; fasten off after last rnd.
Rnd 6: With rs facing, join MC with sl st in center sc of any corner; ch 1, 3 sc in same st as joining, * sc in next 4 sc, Lsc in sc 1 rnd below next sc, Lsc in sc 2 rnds below next sc, Lsc in sc 3 rnds below next sc, Lsc in sc 2 rnds below next sc, Lsc in sc 1 rnd below next sc, (sc in next 9 sc, Lsc in sc 1 rnd below next sc, Lsc in sc 2 rnds below next sc, Lsc in sc 3 rnds below next sc, Lsc in sc 2 rnds below next sc, Lsc in sc 1 rnd below next sc) twice, sc in next 4 sc **, 3 sc in corner sc; rep from * around, ending last rep at **; join with sl st to beg sc; fasten off.
Rnd 7: With rs facing, join CC with sl st in any sc; ch 1, sc in same st as joining and in ea st around working 3 sc in each corner sc; join with sl st to beg sc; fasten off.

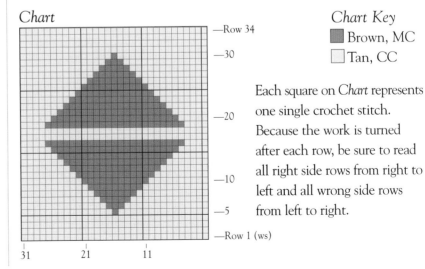

Chart

—Row 34
—30
—20
—10
—5
—Row 1 (ws)

31   21   11

Chart Key
■ Brown, MC
□ Tan, CC

Each square on *Chart* represents one single crochet stitch. Because the work is turned after each row, be sure to read all right side rows from right to left and all wrong side rows from left to right.

Understated Elegance

Intricate but easy crocheted squares frame the center panel of this beautiful afghan. Match the color to a particular decor or, if you prefer, stitch it in white for a wonderful wedding present.

MATERIALS
Worsted-weight yarn, approximately:
30 oz. (1,970 yd.) mauve
Size H crochet hook or size to obtain gauge
Yarn needle

FINISHED SIZE
Approximately 44" x 57"

GAUGE
In pat, 12 dc and 6 rows = 3"
Ea Square = 6¼" square

PATTERN STITCH
Dec: Yo, insert hook in next dc, yo and pull up lp, yo and pull through 2 lps, yo, skip next 2 dc, insert hook in next dc, yo and pull up lp, yo and pull through 2 lps, yo and pull through all 3 lps on hook.

CENTER
Ch 128 loosely.
Row 1 (rs): Dc in 4th ch from hook and in ea ch across [3 skipped chs count as first dc]: 126 dc.
Note: *Mark last row as rs.*
Row 2: Ch 3 [counts as first dc], turn; dc in next dc and in ea dc across.
Rep Row 2 until Center measures approximately 43¾" from beg ch; fasten off after last row.

SQUARES
(Make 28.)
Ch 10, sl st in 1st ch to form ring.
Rnd 1 (rs): Ch 3, 31 dc in ring; join with sl st to top of beg ch: 32 dc.
Note: *Mark last rnd as rs.*
Rnd 2: Ch 7, skip same st as joining and next 3 dc, sl st in next dc, * ch 7, skip next 3 dc, sl st in next dc; rep from * around to last 3 dc, ch 3, skip last 3 dc, tr in same st as joining on prev rnd to form last sp.
Rnd 3: Ch 3, 6 dc in top of last tr made, 7 dc in center ch of ea ch-7 around; join with sl st to top of beg ch-3.
Rnd 4: Sl st in next 3 dc, ch 9, tr in same st as last sl st, * ch 3, skip next dc, dec, ch 3, skip next dc, sc in next dc, ch 3, skip next dc, dec, ch 3, skip next dc **, (tr, ch 5, tr) in next dc; rep from * around, ending last rep at **; join with sl st to 4th ch of beg ch-9.
Rnd 5: Ch 1, sc in same st as joining, * 5 sc in next ch-5 sp, (sc in next st, 3 sc in next ch-3 sp) 4 times **, sc in next tr; rep from * around, ending last rep at **; join with sl st to beg sc.
Rnd 6: Ch 5, skip same st as joining and next 2 sc, * (dc, ch 1, dc) in next sc, ch 2, skip next 2 sc, (dc in next sc, ch 3, skip next 3 sc) 4 times **, dc in next sc, ch 2, skip next 2 sc; rep from * around, ending last rep at **; join with sl st to 3rd ch of beg ch-5.
Rnd 7: Ch 1, sc in same st as joining, * 2 sc in next ch-2 sp, sc in next dc, 3 sc in next ch-1 sp, sc in next dc, 2 sc in next ch-2 sp, (sc in next dc, 3 sc in next ch-3 sp) 4 times **, sc in next dc; rep from * around, ending last rep at **; join with sl st to beg sc; fasten off.

ASSEMBLY
Whipstitch Squares tog, forming 4 strips of 7 squares each. Whipstitch one strip to each long edge of Center and then whipstitch rem strips to each short edge of center.

BORDER
With rs facing, join yarn with sl st in any sc; ch 1, sc evenly around entire afghan working 3 sc in center sc of ea corner; join with sl st to beg sc; fasten off.

Project was stitched with Wool-Ease: Guava #133.

Project was stitched with Al-pa-ka:
Black #153, Oxford Grey #152,
Camel #124, Natural #098.

Father's Day Argyle

Forget argyle socks—instead, give Dad an argyle gift he'll really enjoy!

MATERIALS

Worsted-weight yarn, approximately:
24½ oz. (3,670 yd.) black, MC
10½ oz. (640 yd.) grey, A
10½ oz. (640 yd.) tan, B
3½ oz. (215 yd.) off-white, C
Size I crochet hook or size to
obtain gauge

FINISHED SIZE

Approximately 44" x 53"

GAUGE

In pat, 7 sc and 10 rows = 2"
Note: *To change colors, work last yo of prev st with new color, dropping prev color to ws of work. Fasten off color when no longer needed.*
With MC, ch 150 loosely.
Row 1 (ws): Sc in 2nd ch from hook and in ea ch across.
Row 2 (rs): Ch 1, turn; sc in first sc, change to C, sc in next sc, * change to MC, sc in next 9 sc, change to B, sc in next sc, change to MC, sc in next 9 sc, change to C **, sc in next 2 sc, change to MC, sc in next 9 sc, change to A, sc in next sc, change to MC, sc in next 9 sc, change to C, sc in next 2 sc; rep from * across, ending last rep at **, sc in next sc, change to MC, sc in last sc.
Rows 3–85: Ch 1, turn; cont foll *Chart* as est, repeating sts 23 through 64 for pattern, and reading odd (ws) rows from left to right and even (rs) rows from right to left.

Rows 86–253: Rep Rows 2–85, 2 times.
Row 254: With MC, ch 1, turn; sc in ea sc across; do not fasten off.

BORDER

Rnd 1: Ch 1, turn; sc evenly around working 3 sc in ea corner; join with sl st to beg sc.

Rnds 2–4: Ch 1, do not turn; sc in ea sc around working 3 sc in ea corner; join with sl st to beg sc; fasten off after last rnd.

Rnd 5: With rs facing, join A with sl st in any sc; working from left to right, sc in same st and in ea st around [reverse sc]; join with sl st to beg sc; fasten off.

Chart

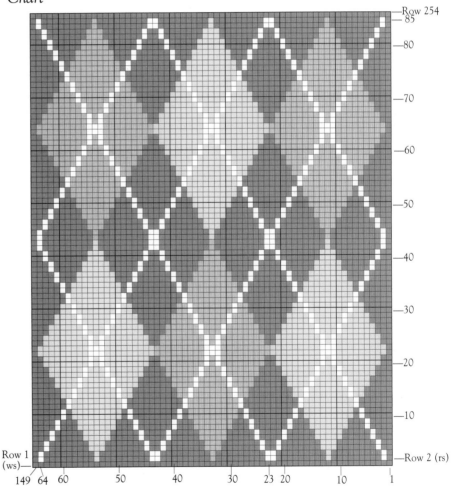

Chart Key ■ Black, MC □ Grey, A □ Tan, B □ Off-White, C

Each square on *Chart* represents one single crochet stitch. Because the work is turned after each row, be sure to read all right side rows from right to left and all wrong side rows from left to right.

Vanna's Signature

This is one of my favorite afghans to make. It's amazing how different the design can look, depending on which yarn I choose. I always make sure to tailor the yarn type and color to the recipient.

MATERIALS

Chunky-weight yarn, approximately:
54 oz. (1,665 yd.) variegated
Size K crochet hook or size to obtain gauge
Yarn needle

FINISHED SIZE

Approximately 42" x 56"

GAUGE

In pat, 5 sc = 2"

PATTERN STITCH

Dec: Pull up a lp in ea of next 2 sts, yo and draw through all 3 lps on hook.

BLOCK

(Make 4.)

Row 1: Ch 2, sc in 2nd ch from hook.

Row 2: Ch 1, turn; 3 sc in sc.

Row 3 (rs): Ch 1, turn; 2 sc in first sc, sc in next sc, 2 sc in last sc: 5 sc.

Note: *Mark last sc made as rs and bottom edge.*

Row 4: Ch 1, turn; sc in ea sc across.

Row 5: Ch 1, turn; sc in first sc, (2 sc in next sc, sc in next sc) twice: 7 sc.

Rows 6 and 7: Ch 1, turn; sc in first sc, 2 sc in next sc, sc in ea sc across to last 2 sc, 2 sc in next sc, sc in last sc: 11 sc.

Row 8: Ch 1, turn; sc in ea sc across.

Rows 9–11: Ch 1, turn; sc in first sc, 2 sc in next sc, sc in ea sc across to last 2 sc, 2 sc in next sc, sc in last sc: 17 sc.

Rep Rows 8–11 until bottom edge measures approximately 19", ending by working Row 8.

Vertical Shaping

Row 1: Ch 1, turn; sc in first sc, 2 sc in next sc, sc in ea sc across to last 3 sc, dec, sc in last sc.

Row 2: Ch 1, turn; sc in first sc, dec, sc in ea sc across to last 2 sc, 2 sc in next sc, sc in last sc.

Row 3: Rep Row 1.

Row 4: Ch 1, turn; sc in ea st across.

Rep Rows 1–4 until longer side edge measures approximately 26", ending by working Row 4.

Horizontal Top Shaping

Rows 1–3: Ch 1, turn; sc in first sc, dec, sc in ea sc across to last 3 sts, dec, sc in last sc.

Row 4: Ch 1, turn; sc in ea st across.

Rep Rows 1–4 until only 5 sts remain, ending by working Row 4.

Next Row: Ch 1, turn; sc in first sc, dec twice.

Last Row: Ch 1, turn; pull up a lp in ea of first 3 sc, yo and draw though all 4 lps on hook; fasten off.

ASSEMBLY

Whipstitch blocks tog as desired, forming 2 strips of 2 blocks ea and matching short edges; then whipstitch strips tog across long edges.

BORDER

Rnd 1 (rs): With rs facing, join yarn with sl st in any corner; ch 1, * 3 sc in corner, sc evenly sp across to next corner; rep from * around; join with sl st to beg sc.

Rnd 2: Ch 1, sc in ea sc around working 3 sc in ea corner sc; join with sl st to beg sc.

Rep Rnd 2 until Border measures approximately 2"; fasten off after last rnd.

Project was stitched with Homespun: Prairie #335.

Flower Patch

For an afghan that's truly different, try this design that combines the structured appearance of geometric shapes with the soft form of flowers.

MATERIALS
Worsted-weight yarn,
   approximately:
18 oz. (1,185 yd.) green, MC
15 oz. (985 yd.) purple, A
6 oz. (395 yd.) red, B
6 oz. (395 yd.) gold, C
Size H crochet hook or size
   to obtain gauge
Yarn needle

FINISHED SIZE
Approximately 48" x 58"

GAUGE
Center = 3¾" diameter
Ea Motif = 10" from point to point

MOTIF
(Make 32.)
Center
With MC, ch 6; join with sl st to form a ring.

Rnd 1 (rs): Ch 3, 23 dc in ring; join with sl st to top of beg ch.

Note: Mark last rnd as rs.

Rnd 2: Ch 1, sc in same st as joining and in front lp only of ea dc around; join with sl st to both lps of beg sc.

Rnd 3: Ch 1, sc in same st as joining, * (hdc, dc, tr) in next sc, (tr, dc, hdc) in next sc **, sc in next sc; rep from * around, ending last rep at **; join with sl st to beg sc; fasten off.

First Block
With rs facing, working behind petals and in free lps of sts on Rnd 1 of Center, join A with sl st in any st, ch 10.

Row 1 (rs): Sc in 2nd ch from hook and in ea ch across.

Rows 2–10: Ch 1, turn; sc in ea sc across; fasten off after last row.

Next 5 Blocks
Block Sequence: B, C, A, B, C. Skip next 3 sts on Rnd 1 of Center from last block made and join next color with sl st in next st, ch 10.

Rows 1–10: Work same as First Block.

Border
Rnd 1: With rs facing, join MC with sl st in first sc of Row 10 of any Block; ch 1, 3 sc in same st as joining, * sc in next 7 sc, pull up a lp in next sc and in end of Row 1 on next block, yo and draw through all 3 lps on hook, work 7 sc evenly sp across to next point **, 3 sc in first sc at point; rep from * around, ending last rep at **; join with sl st to beg sc.

Rnd 2: Ch 1, sc in same st as joining, * 3 sc in next sc, sc in next 8 sc, skip next st **, sc in next 8 sc; rep from * around, ending last rep at **, sc in last 7 sc; join with sl st to beg sc.

Rnd 3: Ch 1, sc in same st as joining and in next sc, * 3 sc in next sc, sc in next 8 sc, skip next 2 sc **, sc in next 8 sc; rep from * around, ending last rep at **, sc in last 6 sc; join with sl st to beg sc; fasten off.

Rnd 4: With rs facing, join A with sl st in 3rd sc of 3-sc group at any point; ch 1, sc in same st as joining and in next 3 sc, * hdc in next 3 sc, dc in next 2 sc, tr in sp before next sc, dc in next 2 sc, hdc in next 3 sc, sc in next 4 sc, ch 1, skip next sc **, sc in next 4 sc; rep from * around, ending last rep at **; join with sl st to beg sc; fasten off.

ASSEMBLY
Holding Motifs with ws tog and keeping block colors running in the same direction, whipstitch Motifs tog, forming 4 strips of 5 Motifs ea and 3 strips of 4 Motifs ea. Then alternating strips, whipstitch strips tog.

EDGING
Rnd 1: With rs facing, join A with sl st in any st; ch 1, sc in same st as joining and in ea sc around working 3 sc in ea point and skipping 1 sc at ea seam; join with sl st to beg sc.

Rnd 2: Ch 1, working from left to right, sc in same st as joining and in ea sc around [reverse sc]; join with sl st to beg sc; fasten off.

Project was stitched with Wool-Ease: Seaspray #123, Lavender #143, Guava #133, Butterscotch #189.

Make a Statement

It's fun to be a little daring with color! Stitch this bold contemporary pattern for an afghan that definitely says, "This is not my grandmother's crochet!"

MATERIALS
Sport-weight yarn,
   approximately:
25 oz. (1,680 yd.) black, MC
10 oz. (670 yd.) green, A
7½ oz. (500 yd.) yellow, B
5 oz. (335 yd.) orange, C
2½ oz. (170 yd.) red, D
Size F crochet hook or size
   to obtain gauge
Yarn needle

FINISHED SIZE
Approximately 45" x 55"

GAUGE
Ea Square = 10"
Rnds 1–5 = 3¾" square

PATTERN STITCH
Dec: * Yo, insert hook in next st, yo and pull up lp, yo and pull through 2 lps on hook; rep from * 2 times more, yo and pull through all 4 lps on hook.

SQUARE (MAKE 20.)
Center
With D, ch 6; join with sl st to form a ring.
Rnd 1 (rs): Ch 3 [counts as first dc throughout], 15 dc in ring; join with sl st to top of beg ch-3.
Rnd 2: Ch 3, 2 dc in same st as joining, * ch 2, skip next dc, dc in next dc, ch 2, skip next dc **, 3 dc in next dc; rep from * around, ending last rep at **; join with sl st to top of beg ch-3.
Rnd 3: Ch 3, 5 dc in next dc, * dc in next dc, (ch 2, dc in next dc) twice, 5 dc in next dc; rep from * 2 times more, (dc in next dc, ch 2) twice; join with sl st to top of beg ch-3; fasten off.
Rnd 4: With rs facing, join C with sl st in same st as joining; ch 3, dc in next 2 dc, * 5 dc in next dc, dc in next 3 dc, ch 2, dc in next dc, ch 2 **, dc in next 3 dc; rep from * around, ending last rep at **; join with sl st to top of beg ch-3.
Rnd 5: Ch 3, dc in next 4 dc, * 5 dc in next dc, dc in next 5 dc, ch 2, dc in next dc, ch 2 **, dc in next 5 dc; rep from * around, ending last rep at **; join with sl st to top of beg ch-3; fasten off.
Rnd 6: With rs facing, join B with sl st in same st as joining; ch 3, dc in next 6 dc, * 5 dc in next dc, dc in next 7 dc, ch 2, dc in next dc, ch 2 **, dc in next 7 dc; rep from * around, ending last rep at **; join with sl st to top of beg ch-3.
Rnd 7: Ch 3, dc in next 8 dc, * 5 dc in next dc, dc in next 9 dc, ch 2, dc in next dc, ch 2 **, dc in next 9 dc; rep from * around, ending last rep at **; join with sl st to top of beg ch-3; fasten off.
Rnd 8: With rs facing, join A with sl st in same st as joining; ch 3, dc in next 10 dc, * 5 dc in next dc, dc in next 11 dc, ch 2, dc in next dc, ch 2 **, dc in next 11 dc; rep from * around, ending last rep at **; join with sl st to top of beg ch-3.
Rnd 9: Ch 3, dc in next 12 dc, * 5 dc in next dc, dc in next 13 dc, ch 2, dc in next dc, ch 2 **, dc in next 13 dc; rep from * around, ending last rep at **; join with sl st to top of beg ch-3; fasten off.
Rnd 10: With rs facing, join MC with sl st in center dc of any corner 5-dc group; ch 3, 2 dc in same st as joining, * dc in next 15 dc, ch 2, dc in next dc, ch 2, dc in next 15 dc **, 3 dc in next dc; repeat from * around, ending last rep at **; join with sl st to top of beg ch-3.

1st Point
Row 1 (ws): Ch 3, turn; dec, dc in next 12 dc, ch 2, dc in next dc, ch 2, dc in next 12 dc, dec, dc in next dc.
Row 2: Ch 3, turn; dec, dc in next 10, ch 2, dc in next dc, →

ch 2, dc in next 10, dec, dc in top of tch.

Row 3: Ch 3, turn; dec, dc in next 8 dc, ch 2, dc in next dc, ch 2, dc in next 8 dc, dec, dc in top of tch.

Row 4: Ch 3, turn; dec, dc in next 6 dc, ch 2, dc in next dc, ch 2, dc in next 6 dc, dec, dc in top of tch.

Row 5: Ch 3, turn; dec, dc in next 4 dc, ch 2, dc in next dc, ch 2, dc in next 4 dc, dec, dc in top of tch.

Row 6: Ch 3, turn; dec, dc in next 2 dc, ch 2, dc in next dc, ch 2, dc in next 2 dc, dec, dc in top of tch.

Row 7: Ch 3, turn; dec, ch 2, dc in next dc, ch 2, skip next ch-2 sp, dec, dc in top of tch.

Row 8: Ch 3, turn; yo, insert hook in next st and pull up lp, yo and pull through 2 lps on hook, yo, insert hook in next ch-2 sp and pull up lp, yo and pull through 2 lps on hook, yo and pull through all 3 lps on hook, dc in next dc, yo, insert hook in next ch-2 sp and pull up lp, yo and pull through 2 lps on hook, yo, insert hook in next st and pull up lp, yo and pull through 2 lps on hook, yo and pull through all 3 lps on hook, dc in top of tch.

Row 9: Ch 2, turn; * yo, insert hook in next st and pull up lp, yo and pull through 2 lps on hook; rep from * 3 times more, yo and pull through all 5 lps on hook; fasten off.

Next 3 Points

Row 1: With ws facing, skip next dc on Rnd 10 from last Point made, join MC with sl st in next dc; ch 3, dec, dc in next 12 dc, ch 2, dc in next dc, ch 2, dc in next 12 dc, dec, dc in next dc.

Rows 2–9: Work same as 1st Point.

ASSEMBLY

Afghan is 4 squares wide by 5 squares long. Whipstitch squares tog.

BORDER

Rnd 1: With rs facing, join MC with sl st in any corner; ch 3, 2 dc in same st as joining, dc evenly sp across to next corner, * 3 dc in corner, dc evenly sp across to next corner; rep from * around; join with sl st to top of beg ch-3; fasten off.

Rnd 2: With rs facing, join A with sl st in any dc; ch 3, dc in ea dc around working 3 dc in ea corner; join with sl st to top of beg ch-3.

Rnds 3 and 4: Ch 3, dc in ea dc around working 3 dc in ea corner; join with sl st to top of beg ch-3; fasten off.

Rnd 5: With rs facing, join MC with sl st in any st; ch 3, dc in ea dc around working 3 dc in ea corner; join with sl st to top of beg ch-3; fasten off.

Selecting colors is one of the best parts of making an afghan like this one.

Set a new mood in an old room with vibrant colors that are sure to brighten anyone's day!

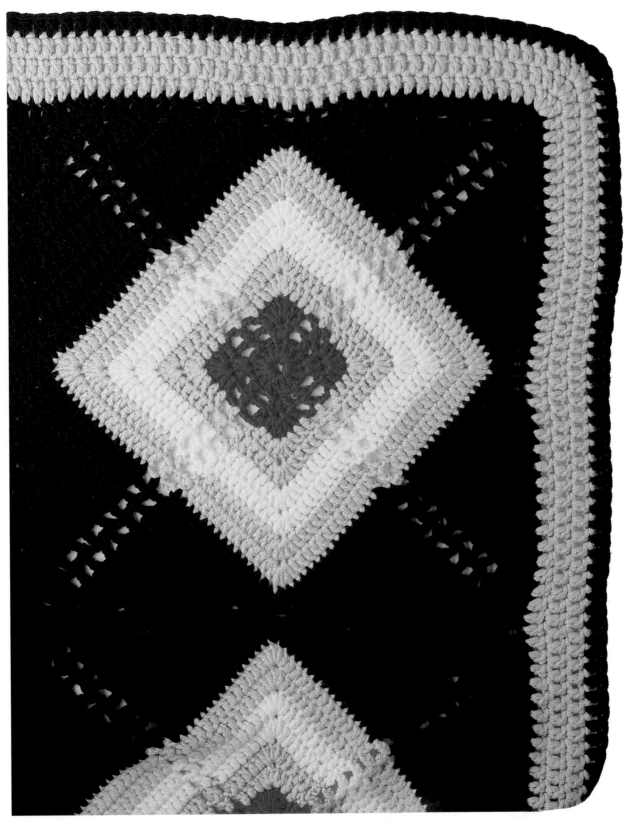

Project was stitched with Microspun: Cherry Red #113, Mango #186, Buttercup #158, Lime #194, Ebony #153.

Winter White Warm-Up

Scalloped borders give this afghan the beauty of a lace doily, while the wool-blend yarn provides a practical warmth.

MATERIALS

Thick and thin textured yarn, approximately:
15 oz. (1,300 yd.) white
Size N crochet hook or size to obtain gauge

FINISHED SIZE

Approximately 49" x 65"

GAUGE

In patt, (dc, ch 1, dc) twice = 2½"

Ch 106.

Row 1 (rs): (Dc, ch 1, dc) in 5th ch from hook, * skip next 2 chs, (dc, ch 1, dc) in next ch; rep from * across to last 2 chs, skip next ch, dc in last ch.

Note: *Mark last row as rs.*

Row 2: Ch 3, turn; (dc, ch 1, dc) in ea ch-1 sp across, skip next dc, dc in next ch.

Rep Row 2 until afghan measures approximately 58" from beg ch, ending by working a ws row.

BORDER

Rnd 1: Ch 1, turn; 3 sc in first dc, * work 67 sc evenly sp across to next corner, 3 sc in corner, work 91 sc evenly sp across end of rows to next corner **, 3 sc in corner; rep from * to ** once; join with sl st to beg sc.

Rnd 2: Ch 1, sc in same st as joining, ch 5, skip next sc, * sc in next sc, (ch 5, skip next 3 sc, sc in next sc) across to center sc of next corner, ch 5, skip next sc; rep from * 2 times more, (sc in next sc, ch 5, skip next 3 sc) across; join with sl st to beg sc.

Rnd 3: Sl st in first ch-5 sp, ch 3, 8 dc in same sp, * sc in next ch-5 sp, ch 5, sc in next ch-5 sp **, 9 dc in next ch-5 sp; rep from * around, ending last rep at **; join with sl st in top of beg ch-3.

Rnd 4: Ch 4, dc in next dc, (ch 1, dc in next dc) 7 times, sc in next ch-5 sp, * dc in next dc, (ch 1, dc in next dc) 8 times, sc in next ch-5 sp; rep from * around; join with sl st to 3rd ch of beg ch-4.

Rnd 5: (Sl st, ch 1, sc) in first ch-1 sp, ch 3, (sc in next ch-1 sp, ch 3) around; join with sl st to beg sc; fasten off.

Classic white will always be in style. You'll find that this winter white afghan adds elegance to any room.

Project was stitched with Woolspun: Natural #098.

Falling Leaves

Present this afghan to the friends who let you use their lake house or to a cousin
who just loves autumn—it's bound to be cherished for years to come.
The color chart makes stitching the swirling leaves a breeze.

MATERIALS
Worsted-weight yarn,
approximately:
35 oz. (1,970 yd.) beige, MC
3½ oz. (160 yd.) gold, A
3½ oz. (160 yd.) brown, B
3½ oz. (160 yd.) red, C
3½ oz. (160 yd.) green, D
Size J crochet hook or size
to obtain gauge

FINISHED SIZE
Approximately 45" x 61"

GAUGE
In patt, 10 sc and 12 rows = 3"

Note: *To change colors, work last yo
of prev st with new color; fasten off
unused color when no longer needed.*

With MC, ch 133 loosely.
Row 1 (rs): Sc in 2nd ch from
hook and in ea ch across: 132 sc.
Note: *Mark last row as rs.*
Rows 2–13: Ch 1, turn; sc in ea
sc across.
Row 14: Ch 1, turn; sc in
first 109 sc, change to A, sc in
next sc, change to MC, sc in last
22 sc.
Rows 15–220: Cont foll *Chart,*
pages 58–59, as est, reading odd
(rs) rows from right to left and
even (ws) rows from left to right;
do not fasten off after last row.

BORDER
Rnd 1 (rs): Ch 1, turn; 3 sc in
first sc, work 129 sc evenly sp
across to last sc, 3 sc in last sc,
work 219 sc evenly sp across end
of rows, working across beg ch,
3 sc in free lp of first ch, work
129 sc evenly sp across to last ch,
3 sc in last ch, work 219 sc evenly sp across end of rows; join
with sl st to beg sc; fasten off:
708 sc.
Rnd 2: With rs facing, join C
with sl st in center sc of any
corner; ch 5, dc in same st as
joining, * ch 1, skip next sc, (dc
in next sc, ch 1, skip next sc)
across to center sc of next corner
**, (dc, ch 2, dc) in center sc;
rep from * around, ending last
rep at **; join with sl st to 3rd
ch of beg ch-5.
Rnd 3: Ch 3, * 5 dc in next corner ch-2 sp, dc in ea dc and ea
ch-1 sp across to next corner
ch-2 sp; rep from * around; join
with sl st to third ch of beg ch-3;
fasten off.
Rnd 4: With rs facing, join B
with sl st in center dc of any
corner; ch 5, dc in same st as
joining, * ch 1, skip next dc, (dc
in next dc, ch 1, skip next dc)
across to center dc of next corner **, (dc, ch 2, dc) in center
dc; rep from * around, ending
last rep at **; join with sl st to
3rd ch of beg ch-5.
Rnd 5: Rep Rnd 3.
Rnd 6: With rs facing, join D
with sl st in 2nd dc of any corner
5-dc group; ch 1, sc in same st as
joining, ch 3, skip next dc, sc in
next dc, ch 3, * (skip next 2 dc,
sc in next dc, ch 3) across to center dc of next corner, skip next
dc, sc in next dc, ch 3; rep from *
2 times more, skip next 2 dc, (sc
in next dc, ch 3, skip next 2 dc)
across; join with sl st to beg sc;
fasten off.

Chart Key

☐ Beige, MC
☐ Gold, A
▨ Brown, B
■ Red, C
▨ Green, D

Each Square on *Chart* represents
one single crochet stitch.
Because the work is turned after
each row, be sure to read all
right side rows from right to left
and all wrong side rows from left
to right. →

*Project was stitched with Wool-Ease: Mushroom #403, Copper
#190, Chestnut Heather #179, Loden #177, Cranberry #138.*

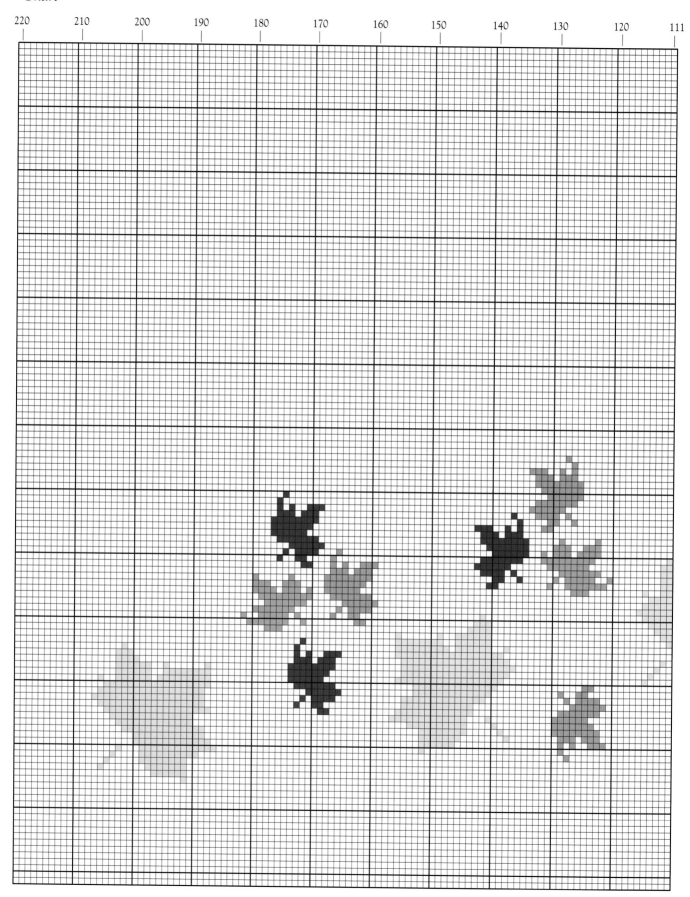

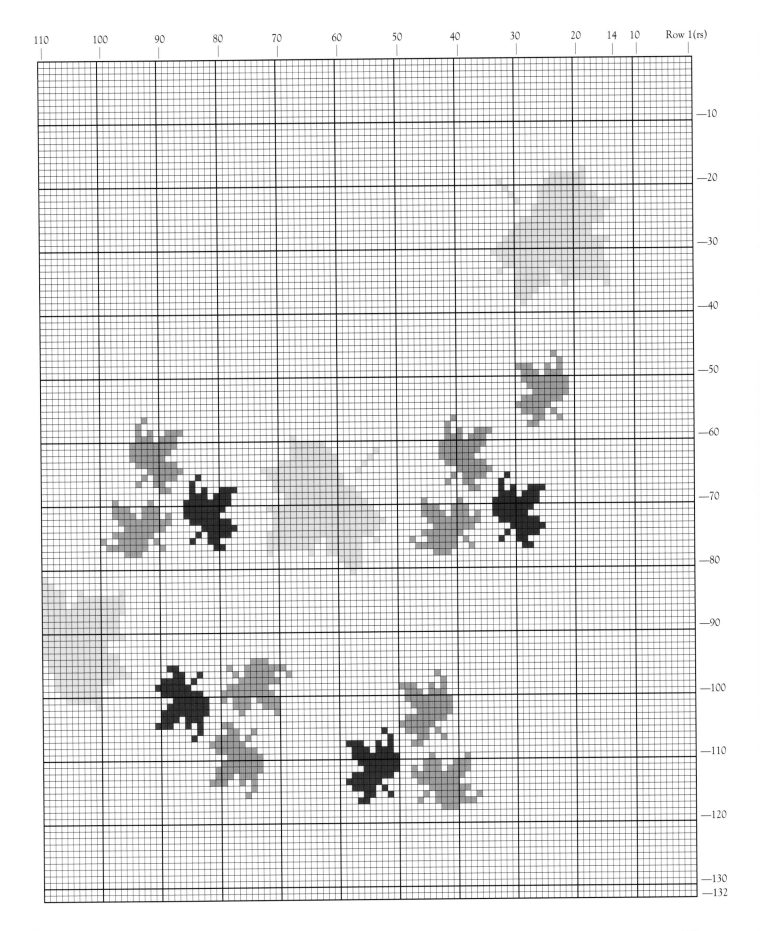

—10

—20

—30

—40

—50

—60

—70

—80

—90

—100

—110

—120

—130
—132

Stripes & Scallops

A simple striped throw takes on a whimsical air when you add loops that are shaped like purse handles.

MATERIALS
Chunky-weight yarn, approximately:
15 oz. (680 yd.) lilac, MC
15 oz. (680 yd.) yellow, CC
Size J crochet hook or size to obtain gauge
2 safety pins

FINISHED SIZE
Approximately 45" x 62"

GAUGE
In patt, 12 sts = 4"

PATTERN STITCH
Long dc (Ldc): Yo, working around next ch-sp, insert hook in st indicated and pull up lp, (yo and draw through 2 lps) twice.

With MC, ch 137 loosely.

Row 1 (rs): Dc in 4th ch from hook and in next ch, * ch 3, skip next 3 chs, dc in next 3 chs; rep from * across; drop lp from hook and place on safety pin.

Note: *Mark last row as rs.*

Row 2: With ws facing, join CC with sl st in first dc; ch 2, skip next 2 dc, * Ldc in next 3 chs 1 row below **, ch 3, skip next 3 dc; rep from * across, ending last rep at **, ch 2, skip next 2 dc, sl st in next ch; drop lp from hook and place on safety pin.

Row 3: With ws facing, pick up MC; ch 3, skip first st, Ldc in next 2 dc 1 row below, * ch 3, skip next 3 dc, Ldc in next 3 sts 1 row below; rep from * across; drop lp from hook and place on safety pin.

Row 4: With rs facing, pick up CC; * ch 3, skip next 3 dc, Ldc in next 3 dc 1 row below; rep from * across to last 3 sts, ch 2, skip next 2 dc, sl st in next ch; drop lp from hook and place on safety pin.

Row 5: With rs facing, pick up MC; ch 3, skip first st, Ldc in next 2 dc 1 row below, * ch 3, skip next 3 dc, Ldc in next 3 sts 1 row below; rep from * across; drop lp from hook and place on safety pin.

Row 6: With ws facing, pick up CC; * ch 3, skip next 3 dc, Ldc in next 3 dc 1 row below; rep from * across to last 3 sts, ch 2, skip next 2 dc, sl st in next ch; drop lp from hook and place on safety pin.

Rep Rows 3–6 until Afghan measures approximately 56" from beg ch, ending by working Row 4; at end of last row fasten off CC.

Last Row: With rs facing, pick up MC; ch 3, skip first st, Ldc in next 2 dc 1 row below, * sc in next 3 dc, Ldc in next 3 sts 1 row below; rep from * across; fasten off.

TOP TRIM
Row 1 (rs): With rs facing and working across last row, join MC with sl st in top of beg ch; ch 3, dc in next 3 sts, (ch 3, skip next 4 sts, dc in next 7 sts) twice, * ch 3, skip next 3 sts, dc in next 7 sts; rep from * 8 times more, ch 3, skip next 4 sts, dc in next 7 sts, ch 3, skip next 4 sts, dc in last 4 sts.

Row 2: Ch 1, turn; sc in first 4 dc, 3 sc in next sp, * sc in next 7 dc, 3 sc in next sp; rep from * across to last 4 sts, sc in last 4 sts; fasten off.

Row 3: With rs facing, join CC with sl st in first sc; ch 1, sc in same st, ch 2, skip next 2 sc, sc in next sc, ch 8, skip next 3 sc, sc in next sc, * ch 5, skip next 5 sc, sc in next sc, ch 8, skip next 3 sc, sc in next sc; rep from * across to last 3 sc, ch 2, skip next 2 sc, sc in last sc.

Row 4: Ch 1, turn; sc in first sc, 19 dc in next ch-8 sp, * sc in next ch-5 sp, 19 dc in next ch-8 sp; rep from * across to last ch-2 sp, skip last ch-2 sp, sc in last sc; fasten off.

BOTTOM TRIM
Row 1 (rs): With rs facing and working across free lps of beg ch, join MC with sl st in first ch; ch 3, dc in next 3 chs, (ch 3, skip next 4 chs, dc in next 7 chs) twice, * ch 3, skip next 3 chs, dc in next 7 chs; rep from * 8 times more, ch 3, skip next 4 chs, dc in next 7 chs, ch 3, skip next 4 chs, dc in last 4 chs.

Rows 2–4: Work same as Top Trim.

Project was stitched with Jiffy: Lilac #144, Pastel Yellow #157.

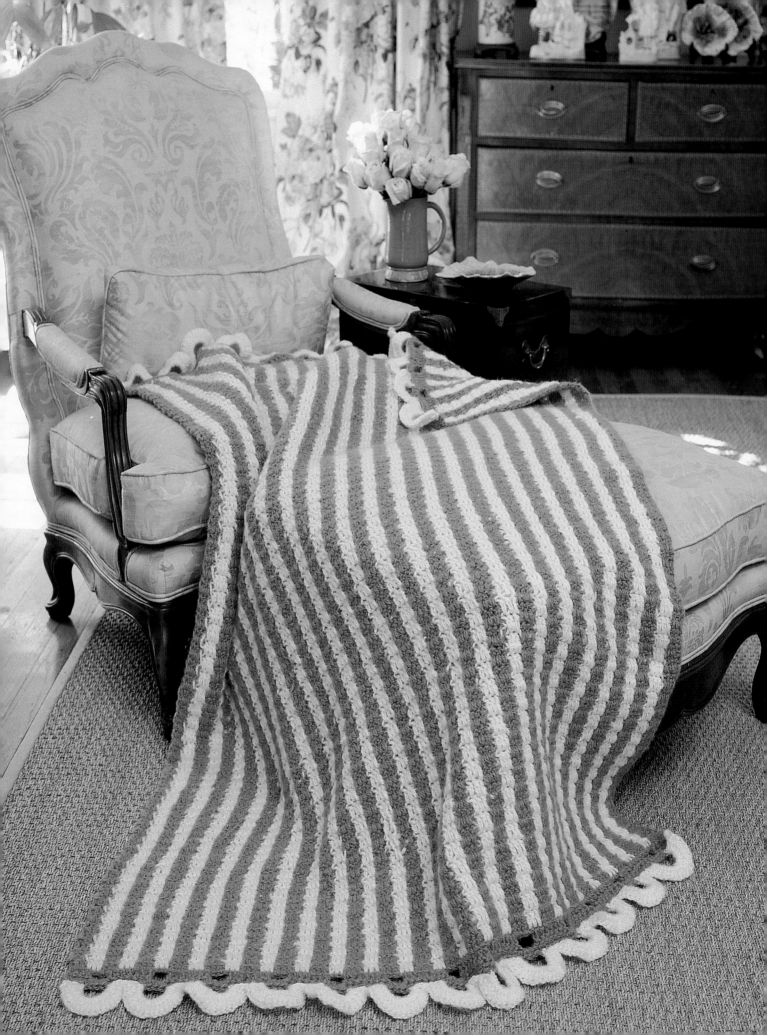

Grey Expectations

This afghan is so chunky and cozy, you'll want to wrap yourself up in it and not emerge until spring! The simple design shows off your favorite color of yarn.

MATERIALS
Chunky-weight yarn, approximately:
42 oz. (755 yd.) grey
Size Q crochet hook or size needed for gauge

FINISHED SIZE
Approximately 48" x 65"

GAUGE
In patt, 3 sts = 2"; 8 rows = 6"

Ch 64.

Row 1 (rs): Sc in 2nd ch from hook, * ch 1, skip next ch, sc in next ch; rep from * across.

Note: *Mark last row as rs.*

Row 2: Ch 3, turn; 2 dc in ea ch-1 sp across, dc in last sc.

Row 3: Ch 1, turn; skip first dc, sc in sp before next dc, * ch 1, skip next 2 dc, sc in sp before next st; rep from * across.

Rep Rows 2 and 3 until Afghan measures approximately 59" from beg ch, ending by working Row 3.

BORDER
Rnd 1 (rs): Ch 1, do not turn; 2 sc in end of last row made, * work 85 sc evenly sp across end of rows to next corner, 3 sc in corner, work 61 sc evenly across to next corner **, 3 sc in corner; rep from * to ** once, sc in same st as beg sc; join with sl st to beg sc.

Rnd 2: Dc in same st as joining, * ch 3, 4 dc around post of last dc made, skip next 3 sc **, dc in next sc; rep from * around, ending last rep at **; join with sl st to beg dc; fasten off.

Project was stitched with Wool-Ease Thick & Quick: Pewter #152.

Zigzags

If you're looking for an afghan that can be stitched up quickly and easily, this is a good choice. Consider using two complementary variegated colors. Or if you prefer, use a solid yarn and a variegated yarn that contains flecks of the solid color.

MATERIALS
Chunky-weight yarn, approximately:
24 oz. (740 yd.) blue, MC
24 oz. (740 yd.) variegated, CC
Size J crochet hook or size to obtain gauge

FINISHED SIZE
Approximately 40" x 58"

GAUGE
In patt, point to point = 4½";
4 rows = 1¾"

Note: *To change colors, work last yo of prev st with new color; fasten off old color.*

With MC, ch 152 loosely.
Row 1 (rs): Sc in 2nd ch from hook and in next 6 chs, * 3 sc in next ch, sc in next 7 chs **, skip next 2 chs, sc in next 7 chs; rep from * across, ending last rep at **.
Rows 2–4: Ch 1, turn; skip first sc, working in bk lps only, sc in next 7 sc, 3 sc in next sc, * sc in next 7 sc, skip next 2 sc, sc in next 7 sc, 3 sc in next sc; rep from * across to last 8 sc, sc in next 6 sc, skip next sc, sc in last sc; at end of last row change to CC.

Rows 5–8: Ch 1, turn; skip first sc, working in bk lps only, sc in next 7 sc, 3 sc in next sc, * sc in next 7 sc, skip next 2 sc, sc in next 7 sc, 3 sc in next sc; rep from * across to last 8 sc, sc in next 6 sc, skip next sc, sc in last sc; at end of last row change to MC.
Rows 9–12: Ch 1, turn; skip first sc, working in bk lps only, sc in next 7 sc, 3 sc in next sc, * sc in next 7 sc, skip next 2 sc, sc in next 7 sc, 3 sc in next sc; rep from * across to last 8 sc, sc in next 6 sc, skip next sc, sc in last sc; at end of last row change to CC.
Rows 13–132: Rep Rows 5–12, 15 times; at end of last row do not change colors; fasten off.

Project was stitched with Homespun: Barrington #336, Tudor #315.

Pools of Blue

This serene aqua throw is perfect for a beach house—or for just curling up on your lounge chair and watching the sunrise.

MATERIALS

Worsted-weight yarn, approximately:
16 oz. (1,425 yd.) aqua, MC
10 oz. (895 yd.) blue, A
3 oz. (540 yd.) white, B
Size N crochet hook or size to obtain gauge
Yarn needle

FINISHED SIZE

Approximately 45" x 59"

Note: *Afghan is stitched holding 2 strands of yarn tog throughout.*

GAUGE

In patt, 2 sc = 1"; 3 rows = 1¾"
Ea Strip = 9" wide

PATTERN STITCH

Dec: Pull up a lp in ea of first 2 sts or next 2 sts, yo and draw through all 3 lps on hook.

Note: *To change colors, work last yo of prev st with new color; fasten off unused color.*

Strip 1 (Make 3.)

With 1 strand ea of MC and A, ch 24 loosely.
Row 1 (rs): Insert hook in 2nd ch from hook and pull up lp, insert hook in next ch and pull up lp, yo and draw through all 3 lps on hook, sc in next 9 chs, 3 sc in next ch, sc in next 9 chs, dec.
Note: *Mark last row as rs and bottom edge.*
Rows 2–6: Ch 1, turn; dec, sc in next 9 sc, 3 sc in next sc, sc in next 9 sc, dec; at the end of last row change to 1 strand ea of MC and B.
Rows 7–12: Ch 1, turn; dec, sc in next 9 sc, 3 sc in next sc, sc in next 9 sc, dec; at the end of last row change to 1 strand ea of MC and A.
Rows 13–18: Ch 1, turn; dec, sc in next 9 sc, 3 sc in next sc, sc in next 9 sc, dec; at the end of last row change to 1 strand ea of MC and B.
Rows 19–90: Rep Rows 7–18, 6 times; fasten off after last row.

Strip 2 (Make 2.)

With 1 strand ea of MC and A, ch 24 loosely.
Row 1 (rs): Insert hook in 2nd ch from hook and pull up lp, insert hook in next ch and pull up lp, yo and draw through all 3 lps on hook, sc in next 9 chs, 3 sc in next ch, sc in next 9 chs, dec.
Note: *Mark last row as rs and bottom edge.*
Row 2: Ch 1, turn; dec, sc in next 9 sc, 3 sc in next sc, sc in next 9 sc, dec, change to 1 strand ea of MC and B.
Rows 3 and 4: Ch 1, turn; dec, sc in next 9 sc, 3 sc in next sc, sc in next 9 sc, dec; at the end of last row change to 1 strand ea of MC and A.
Rows 5 and 6: Ch 1, turn; dec, sc in next 9 sc, 3 sc in next sc, sc in next 9 sc, dec; at the end of last row change to 1 strand ea of MC and B.
Rows 7–90: Rep Rows 3–6, 21 times; fasten off after last row.

ASSEMBLY

Strip Sequence: Strip 1, (Strip 2, Strip 1) twice.

With 2 strands of MC, hold 2 Strips with ws tog, bottom edges at same end, and working across end of rows, join yarn with sl st in end of Row 1; ch 1, sc in same sp as joining and in end of ea row across; fasten off. Repeat for remaining Strips.

EDGING

With 2 strands of MC, join yarn with sl st in any point; ch 1, sc evenly around entire afghan working 3 sc in each point and 2 sc in ea corner; join with sl st to beg sc; fasten off.

Project was stitched with Imagine: Aqua #102, Moody Blues #328, White #100.

Crisscross

This plush two-tone afghan is a luxurious accent for a formal bedroom.

MATERIALS
Chunky-weight yarn,
approximately:
(600 yd.) black, MC
(600 yd.) white, CC
Size P crochet hook or size
to obtain gauge

FINISHED SIZE
Approximately 40" x 56"

GAUGE
In pat, 3 sts = 2"

PATTERN STITCH
Split treble crochet (split tr):
Yo twice, working around previous row, insert hook in same sp as last st worked 2 rows below, yo and pull up a lp even with lp on hook, (yo and pull through 2 lps on hook) twice, yo twice, insert hook in next ch-1 sp 2 rows below, yo and pull up a lp, (yo and pull through 2 lps on hook) twice, yo and pull through all 3 lps on hook.

With MC, ch 60 loosely.
Row 1 (rs): Sc in 2nd ch from hook and in next 2 chs, * ch 1, skip next ch, sc in next 3 chs; rep from * across.

Note: Mark last row as rs.
Row 2: Ch 3 [counts as first dc throughout], turn; dc in next sc and in ea sc and in ea ch across; fasten off.
Row 3: With rs facing, join CC with sl st in first dc; ch 1, sc in same st as joining, working around prev row, tr in first ch-1 sp 2 rows below, skip next dc from last sc worked, sc in next dc, * ch 1, skip next dc, sc in next dc **, work split tr, skip next dc from last sc worked, sc in next dc; rep from * across, ending last rep at **, working around prev row, tr in same sp as second leg of last split tr made, sc in top of tch.
Row 4: Ch 3, turn; dc in next tr and in ea st and in ea ch across; fasten off.
Row 5: With rs facing, join MC with sl st in first dc; ch 1, sc in same st as joining, working around prev row, tr in first ch-1 sp 2 rows below, skip next dc from last sc worked, sc in next dc, * ch 1, skip next dc, sc in next dc **, work split tr, skip next dc from last sc worked, sc in next dc; rep from * across, ending last rep at **, working around prev row, tr in same sp as second leg of last split tr made, sc in top of tch.
Row 6: Ch 3, turn; dc in next tr and in ea st and in ea ch across; fasten off.
Rep Rows 3–6 until afghan measures approximately 58", ending by working Row 5; do not fasten off.

BORDER
Rnd 1: Ch 3, do not turn; dc evenly around entire afghan working 3 dc in each corner; join with sl st in top of beg ch-3; fasten off.
Rnd 2: With rs facing, join CC with sl st in any dc; ch 1, working from left to right, sc in same st and in ea dc around [reverse sc]; join with sl st to beg sc; fasten off.

If you stitched this afghan with chenille, be sure to hand-wash it.

Project was stitched with Chenille Thick & Quick: Black #153, Antique White #098.

Ode to the Amish

In the Amish tradition, this afghan makes wonderful use of bold solids framed with black. Be sure to keep an eye on the Assembly Diagram when joining the blocks so that each row of color will match.

MATERIALS

Worsted-weight yarn, approximately:

24 oz. (1,600 yd.) black, MC
6 oz. (400 yd.) dark rose, A
3 oz. (200 yd.) rose, B
3 oz. (200 yd.) hunter green, C
3 oz. (200 yd.) green, D
3 oz. (200 yd.) dark purple, E
3 oz. (200 yd.) purple, F
Size H crochet hook or size to obtain gauge
Yarn needle

FINISHED SIZE

Approximately 43" x 64"

GAUGE

Ea Square = 5"

PATTERN STITCH

Picot: Ch 4, sl st in 4th ch from hook.

Square 1 (Make 33.)

With B, ch 6; join with sl st to form ring.

Rnd 1 (rs): Ch 3 [counts as first dc throughout], 15 dc in ring; join with sl st to top of beg ch.
Note: *Mark last rnd as rs.*
Rnd 2: Ch 4, (dc in next dc, ch 1) around; join with sl st to 3rd ch of beg ch-4; fasten off.

Rnd 3: With rs facing, join A with sl st in any ch-1 sp; ch 3, 2 dc in same ch-1 sp, ch 1, (3 dc in next ch-1 sp, ch 1) around; join with sl st in top of beg ch-3; fasten off.
Rnd 4: With rs facing, join MC with sl st in any ch-1 sp; ch 1, sc in same ch-1 sp, ch 4, sc in next ch-1 sp, * (ch 3, sc in next ch-1 sp) 3 times, ch 4, sc in next ch-1 sp; rep from * 2 times more, ch 3, (sc in next ch-1 sp, ch 3) twice; join with sl st to beg sc.
Rnd 5: Sl st in first ch-4 sp, (ch 3, 2 dc, ch 2, 3 dc) in same ch-4 sp, * ch 1, 3 hdc in next ch-3 sp, ch 1, 3 sc in next ch-3 sp, ch 1, 3 hdc in next ch-3 sp, ch 1 **, (3 dc, ch 2, 3 dc) in next ch-4 sp; rep from * around, ending last rep at **; join with sl st to top of beg ch-3.
Rnd 6: Ch 1, sc in same st as joining and in next 2 dc, (2 sc, ch 2, 2 sc) in next ch-2 sp, * sc in next 3 dc, (skip next ch, sc in next 3 sts) 4 times, (2 sc, ch 2, 2 sc) in next ch-2 sp; rep from * 2 times more, (sc in next 3 sts, skip next ch) 4 times; join with sl st to beg sc; fasten off.

Square 2 (Make 27.)

With D, work same as ➜

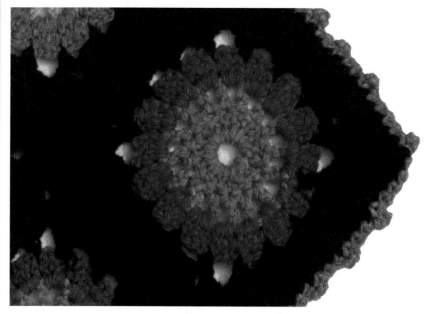

Project was stitched with Wool-Ease: Black #153, Dark Rose Heather #139, Rose Heather #140, Hunter Green #132, Green Heather #130, Plum #145, Grape Heather #144.

Square 1 through Rnd 2.
Rnd 3: With C, work same as Square 1.
Rnds 4–6: Work same as Square 1.

Square 3 (Make 33.)
With F, work same as Square 1 through Rnd 2.
Rnd 3: With E, work same as Square 1.
Rnds 4–6: Work same as Square 1.

ASSEMBLY
Referring to *Assembly Diagram,* whipstitch squares tog.

BORDER
Rnd 1: With rs facing and referring to *Assembly Diagram,* join MC with sl st in corner ch-2 sp; ch 1, 2 sc in same ch-2 sp, * work 36 sc evenly sp across to next corner ch-2 sp, 3 sc in corner ch-2 sp, (sc in next 18 sc, skip next 2 sc, sc in next 18 sc, 3 sc in next ch-2 sp) 7 times, work 36 sc evenly sp across to next corner ch-2 sp **, 3 sc in corner ch-2 sp, (sc in next 18 sc, skip next 2 sc, sc in next 18 sc, 3 sc in next ch-2 sp) 4 times; rep from * to ** once, (3 sc in next ch-2 sp, sc in next 18 sc, skip next 2 sc, sc in next 18 sc) 4 times, sc in same sp as beg sc; join with sl st to beg sc; fasten off.
Rnd 2: With rs facing, join A with sl st in same st as joining; ch 1, (sc, picot, sc) in same st as joining, * sc in next 3 sc, picot, (sc in next 4 sc, picot) 8 times,

Assembly Diagram

~Beg Border

sc in next 3 sc, [(sc, picot, sc) in next sc, sc in next 3 sc, picot, (sc in next 4 sc, picot) 3 times, sc in next 3 sc, skip next 2 sc, sc in next 3 sc, picot, (sc in next 4 sc, picot) 3 times, sc in next 3 sc] 7 times, (sc, picot, sc) in next sc, sc in next 3 sc, picot, (sc in next 4 sc, picot) 8 times, sc in next 3 sc, [(sc, picot, sc) in next sc, sc

in next 3 sc, picot, (sc in next 4 sc, picot) 3 times, sc in next 3 sc, skip next 2 sc, sc in next 3 sc, picot, (sc in next 4 sc, picot) 3 times, sc in next 3 sc] 4 times **, (sc, picot, sc) in next sc; rep from * to ** once; join with sl st to beg sc; fasten off.

Playful Plaid

This happy pattern works equally well as a baby blanket or as a play pallet for my nephew Crawford. Stitched in a fine acrylic yarn, it is lightweight and extra soft. Refer to page 116 to make the sweater my daughter, Giovanna, is wearing.

Projects were stitched with Microspun: Lily White #100, Buttercup #158, Lime #194, Lilac #144.

AFGHAN

MATERIALS

Sport-weight acrylic yarn, approximately:

15 oz. (1,010 yd.) white, MC

7½ oz. (505 yd.) yellow, A

2½ oz. (170 yd.) green, B

2½ oz. (170 yd.) lilac, C

Size H crochet hook or size to obtain gauge

FINISHED SIZE

Approximately 39" x 46"

GAUGE

In pat, 11 sc and 12 rows = 3"

Note: To change colors, work last yo of prev st with new color, dropping prev color to ws of work.

With MC, ch 124.

Row 1 (rs): Sc in 2nd ch from hook and in next 17 chs, * (change to A, sc in next ch, change to MC) 5 times, change to B, sc in next 3 chs, (change to MC, sc in next ch, change to A, sc in next ch) 5 times, change to MC **, sc in next 20 chs, change to B, sc in next ch, change to MC, sc in next 20 chs; rep from * to ** once, sc in last 18 chs: 123 sc.

Note: Mark last row as rs.

Row 2: Ch 1, turn; reading *Chart*, page 75, from left to right, sc in first 19 sc, * (change to A, sc in next sc, change to MC) 5 times, change to C, sc in next sc, (change to MC, sc in next sc, change to A, sc in next sc) 5 times, change to MC **, sc in next 21 sc, change to C, sc in next sc, change to MC, sc in next 21 sc; rep from * to ** once, sc in last 19 sc.

Row 3: Ch 1, turn; reading *Chart* from right to left, sc in first 18 sc, * (change to A, sc in next sc, change to MC) 5 times, change to B, sc in next 3 sc, (change to MC, sc in next sc, change to A, sc in next sc) 5 times, change to MC **, sc in next 20 sc, change to B, sc in next sc, change to MC, sc in next 20 sc; rep from * to ** once, sc in last 18 sc.

Rows 4–82: Cont foll *Chart* as est, reading even (ws) rows from left to right and odd (rs) rows from right to left.

Rows 83–162: Cont foll *Chart* as est, rep Rows 1–80 once; fasten off at end of last row.

BORDER

Rnd 1: With rs facing, join C with sl st in any corner; ch 1, 3 sc in same st as joining, sc evenly around working 3 sc in ea corner; join with sl st to beg sc.

Rnds 2 and 3: Ch 1, do not turn; sc in same st as joining and in ea sc around working 3 sc in ea corner sc; join with sl st to beg sc; fasten off after last rnd.

Rnd 4: With rs facing, join MC with sl st in any sc; ch 1, sc in same st as joining and in ea sc around working 3 sc in ea corner sc; join with sl st to beg sc.

Rnds 5–8: Ch 1, sc in same st as joining and in ea sc around working 3 sc in ea corner sc; join with sl st to beg sc; fasten off after last rnd.

Rnd 9: With rs facing, join B with sl st in any sc; ch 1, sc in same st as joining and in ea sc around working 3 sc in ea corner sc; join with sl st to beg sc.

Rnds 10 and 11: Ch 1, sc in same st as joining and in ea sc around working 3 sc in ea corner sc; join with sl st to beg sc; fasten off after last rnd.

Chart Key

☐ White, MC

☐ Yellow, A

☐ Green, B

☐ Lilac, C

Each Square on *Chart* represents one single crochet stitch. Because the work is turned after each row, be sure to read all right side rows from right to left and all wrong side rows from left to right.

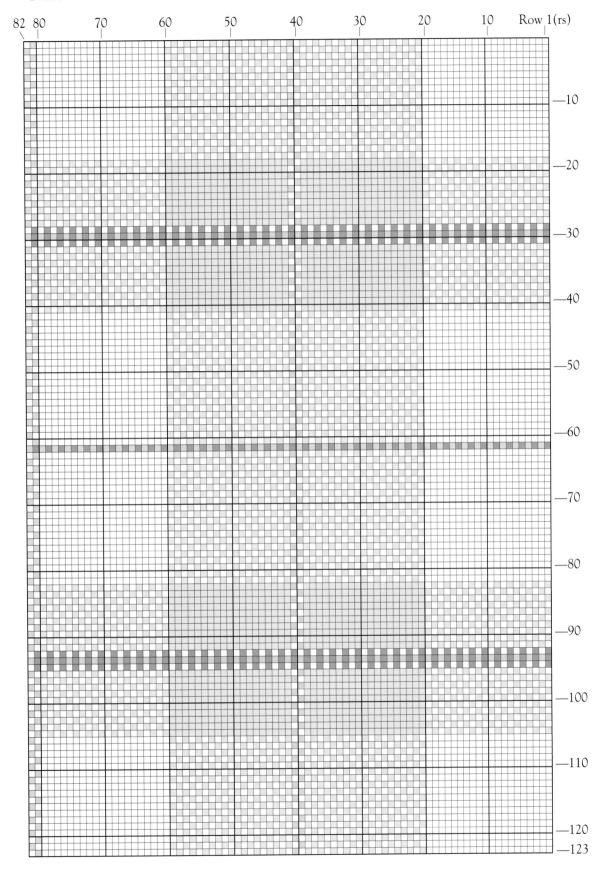

Basketweave Bundle of Joy

A newborn loves to be kept warm and cozy, and this afghan will do just that. If you're not sure whether the baby will be a boy or a girl, stitch the blanket in the colors shown here for an all-purpose baby gift.

MATERIALS

Sport-weight yarn, approximately:
10 oz. (920 yd.) yellow, MC
10 oz. (920 yd.) green, A
10 oz. (920 yd.) pink, B
10 oz. (920 yd.) blue, C
Sizes N and K crochet hooks or sizes to obtain gauge

FINISHED SIZE

Approximately 35" x 40"

GAUGE

In pat with larger hook, 13 sts and 10 rows = 5"

Note: *Afghan is stitched holding 2 strands of yarn tog throughout. To change colors, work last yo of prev st with new color; fasten off old color.*

PATTERN STITCHES

Front Post dc (FPdc): Yo, insert hook from front to back around post of st indicated, yo and pull up lp, (yo and pull through 2 lps) twice, sk st behind FPdc.

Back Post dc (BPdc): Yo, insert hook from back to front around post of st indicated, yo and pull up lp, (yo and pull through 2 lps) twice; sk st in front of BPdc.

With larger hook and MC, ch 90.
Row 1 (rs): Dc in 4th ch from hook and in ea ch across: 88 sts.
Note: *Mark last row as rs.*
Row 2: Ch 2, turn; skip first dc, * BPdc around next 2 dc, FPdc around next 4 dc; rep from * across, BPdc around last 3 sts, change to A.
Row 3: Ch 2, turn; skip first BPdc, BPdc around next 3 sts, * FPdc around next 2 FPdc, BPdc around next 4 sts; rep from * across.
Row 4: Ch 2, turn; skip first BPdc, FPdc around next 3 BPdc, * BPdc around next 2 FPdc, FPdc around next 4 sts; rep from * across, change to B.
Row 5: Ch 2, turn; skip first FPdc, * FPdc around next 2 FPdc **, BPdc around next 4 sts; rep from * across, ending last rep at **, BPdc around last st.
Row 6: Ch 2, turn; skip first BPdc, * BPdc around next 2 FPdc, FPdc around next 4 BPdc; rep from * across, BPdc

around last 3 sts, change to C.
Rows 7 and 8: Rep Rows 3 and 4, changing to MC in last st on last row.
Rows 9 and 10: Rep Rows 5 and 6, changing to A in last st on last row.
Rows 11–68: Rep Rows 3–10, 7 times, then rep Rows 3 and 4 once; do not fasten off.

BORDER

Rnd 1 (rs): With smaller hook, ch 1, turn; 3 sc in first BPdc, sc in ea st across to corner, * 3 sc in corner, sc evenly across to next corner; rep from * around; join with sl st to beg sc.
Rnd 2: Ch 1, turn; sc in same st as joining and in ea sc around working 3 sc in ea corner sc; join with sl st to beg sc.
Rnd 3: Ch 1, do not turn; sc in same st as joining and in ea sc around working 3 sc in ea corner sc; join with sl st to beg sc; fasten off.

Project was stitched with Babysoft: Pastel Yellow #157, Pastel Green #156, Pastel Pink #101, Pastel Blue #106.

Baby Lace

There is nothing lovelier than a new life. And the delicate stitches in this blanket complement a baby's exquisite beauty.

MATERIALS
Worsted-weight yarn, approximately:
23 oz. (1,460 yd.) white
Size G crochet hook or size to obtain gauge
Yarn needle

FINISHED SIZE
Approximately 37" x 48"

GAUGE
In pat, one rep = 2¾"

Ch 134.
Row 1 (ws): Sc in 2nd ch from hook, * ch 5, skip next 3 chs, sc in next ch; rep from * across: 33 ch-5 sps.
Row 2: Ch 6, turn; sc in first ch-5 sp, * 7 dc in next ch-5 sp, sc in next ch-5 sp **, ch 5, sc in next ch-5 sp; rep from * across, ending last rep at **, ch 2, tr in last sc.
Row 3: Ch 1, turn; sc in first tr, ch 5, skip next ch-2 sp and next 2 sts, * sc in next dc, ch 5, skip next 3 dc, sc in next dc, ch 5 **, sc in next ch-5 sp, ch 5, skip next 2 sts; rep from * across, ending last rep at **, skip next 2 sts and next 2 chs, sc in next ch.
Rep Rows 2 and 3 until afghan measures approximately 42" from beg, ending by working Row 2.
Last Row: Ch 1, turn; sc in first tr, ch 3, skip next ch-2 sp and next 2 sts, * sc in next dc, ch 3, skip next 3 dc, sc in next dc, ch 3 **, sc in next ch-5 sp, ch 3, skip next 2 sts; rep from * across, ending last rep at **, skip next 2 sts and next 2 chs, sc in next ch; fasten off.

BORDER
Row 1: Ch 5, (3 dc, ch 2, 3 dc, tr) in 5th ch from hook.
Row 2: Ch 4, turn; (3 dc, ch 2, 3 dc) in next ch-2 sp, skip next 3 dc, tr in next ch.
Rows 3–224: Ch 4, turn; (3 dc, ch 2, 3 dc) in next ch-2 sp, skip next 3 dc, tr in next ch.

Scallop
Row 1: Ch 2, do not turn; working across end of rows, skip first row, * tr in next row, (ch 1, tr in same row) 8 times, ch 2, skip next row, sc in next row **, ch 2, skip next row; rep from * across, ending last rep at **.
Row 2: Ch 3, turn; * sl st in next sp, (ch 3, sl st in next st) 9 times; rep from * across; fasten off.

FINISHING
Sew Border to afghan, keeping scallops to outside edge and wrapping 1 scallop around each corner, 11 scallops along each short edge, and 15 scallops along each long edge.

The innocence of a baby is one of life's most amazing treasures. Make this afghan for a friend who's expecting and then wait to see how beautiful her baby looks wrapped up in your gift.

Project was stitched with Wool-Ease: White/Multi #301.

Pink Perfection

I love this sweet floral pattern. The afghan not only works well for wrapping a baby girl, but also is decorative enough to use as a bedding coverlet for a big girl like Giovanna.

MATERIALS

Sport-weight yarn,
approximately:
20 oz. (1,835 yd.) pink
Size G crochet hook or size
to obtain gauge
Yarn needle

FINISHED SIZE

Approximately 39" x 49"

GAUGE

In patt, 9 dc = 2"; 7 rows = 3"
Ea Motif = 5" square

PATTERN STITCH

Knot St: Pull up a ¼" long lp on hook, ch 1, sc in back ridge of ch just made.

Motifs (Make 12.)

Center
Ch 6; join with sl st to form a ring.
Rnd 1 (rs): Ch 5 [counts as first dc plus ch-2], (dc, ch 2) 7 times in ring; join with sl st to 3rd ch of beg ch-5.
Note: *Mark last rnd as rs.*
Rnd 2: Ch 1, (sc, hdc, 3 dc, hdc, sc) in ea ch-2 sp around; join with sl st to beg sc.
Rnd 3: Ch 1, working behind petals, sc in same st as joining on Rnd 1, ch 3, * sc in next dc on

Rnd 1, ch 3; rep from * around; join with sl st to beg sc.
Rnd 4: Ch 1, (sc, hdc, 5 dc, hdc, sc) in ea ch-3 sp around; join with sl st to beg sc.
Rnd 5: Ch 1, working behind petals, sc in same st as joining on Rnd 3, ch 4, * sc in next sc on Rnd 3, ch 4; rep from * around; join with sl st to beg sc.
Rnd 6: Ch 1, (sc, hdc, 9 dc, hdc, sc) in ea ch-4 sp around; join with sl st to beg sc; do not fasten off.

Leaves

1st 3-Leaf Group: * Ch 6, sc in 2nd ch from hook, hdc in next ch, dc in next 3 chs **, sc in same st as joining on Rnd 6; rep from * once more, then rep from * to ** once, sl st in same st as

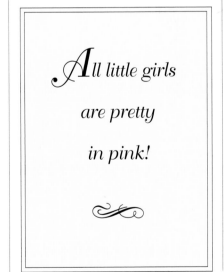

All little girls are pretty in pink!

joining on Rnd 6; fasten off.
Next 3-Leaf Group: With rs of Center facing, skip next 2 petals from last 3-leaf group made, join yarn with sl st in sp before next petal, * ch 6, sc in 2nd ch from hook, hdc in next ch, dc in next 3 chs **, sc in same sp as joining on Rnd 6; rep from * once more, then rep from * to ** once, sl st in same sp as joining on Rnd 6; fasten off.
Rep next 3-leaf group 2 times more.

Trim

Rnd 1: With rs facing, join yarn with sl st in tip of first leaf of any 3-leaf group; * ch 2, (2 dc, ch 3, 2 dc) in tip of next leaf, ch 2, sl st in tip of next leaf, ch 3, skip next petal, tr in sp before next petal, ch 3 **, sl st in tip of next leaf; rep from * around, ending last rep at **; join with sl st to beg sl st.
Rnd 2: Ch 3, * dc in next ch-2 sp and in next dc, skip next dc, (2 dc, ch 3, 2 dc) in next ch-3 sp, skip next dc, dc in next dc and in next ch-2 sp, (dc in next st, 2 dc in next ch-3 sp) twice **, dc in next sl st; rep from * around, ending last rep at **; join with sl st to top ch of beg ch-3; fasten off. ➜

Project was stitched with Babysoft: Pastel Pink #101.

AFGHAN BODY

Ch 47 loosely.

Row 1 (rs): Dc in 4th ch from hook and in ea ch across: 45 sts.

Note: *Mark last row as rs.*

Row 2: Ch 3 [counts as first dc throughout], turn; skip first dc, dc in next dc and in ea dc across, dc in next ch.

Rows 3–15: Ch 3, turn; skip first dc, dc in next dc and in ea dc across.

Row 16: Ch 25, dc in 4th ch from hook and in ea ch across, turn; dc in ea dc across afghan body; fasten off; with yarn, ch 25, dc in 4th ch from hook and in each ch across.

Row 17: Ch 3, turn; skip first dc, dc in next dc and in ea dc across, with rs of afghan body facing, dc in ea dc across.

Rows 18–31: Rep Rows 3–16.

Row 32: Ch 3, turn; skip first dc, dc in next dc and in ea dc across, with ws of afghan body facing, dc in ea dc across.

Rows 33–65: Ch 3, turn; skip first dc, dc in next dc and in ea dc across.

Row 66: Ch 1, turn; sl st in first 24 dc, ch 3, dc in next dc and in ea dc across to last 23 dc, leave last 23 dc unworked.

Rows 67–80: Ch 3, turn; skip first dc, dc in next dc and in ea dc across.

Rows 81–95: Rep Rows 66–80; fasten off at end of last row. Sew 3 Motifs in ea corner of afghan.

BORDER

Rnd 1 (rs): With rs facing, join yarn with sl st in any corner ch-3 sp; ch 1, 5 sc in same sp as joining, * work 128 sc evenly sp across to next corner ch-3 sp, 5 sc in corner ch-3 sp, work 173 sc evenly sp across to next corner ch-3 sp **, 5 sc in corner ch-3 sp; rep from * to ** once; join with sl st to beg sc.

Rnd 2: Ch 1, sc in same st as joining; * (work 2 knot sts, sc in next sc) 4 times **, (work 2 knot sts, skip next 2 sc, sc in next sc) across to 2nd sc of next corner 5-sc group; rep from * 2 times more, then rep from * to ** once, (work 2 knot sts, skip next 2 sc, sc in next sc) across to last 2 sc, work knot st, skip last 2 sc, tr in beg sc to form last sp.

Rnds 3–10: Ch 1, sc around post of last tr made, (work 2 knot sts, sc in next knot st sp) around, work knot st, tr in beg sc to form last sp; fasten off at end of last rnd.

Welcome Home, Baby

Stitch these clever handmade baby gifts to show your expectant friend how happy you are for her.
The crocheted wreath and matching picture frame are sure to be big hits at her shower!

WREATH

MATERIALS

Sport-weight yarn,
approximately:
1¾ oz. (195 yd.) variegated
Size G crochet hook
7"-diameter ring
Polyester batting
2 yd. ea ³⁄₁₆"-wide picot-edged
ribbons: pink, blue, white
Various baby trinkets
Craft glue
Yarn needle

FINISHED SIZE
Approximately 8¼" diameter

Row 1: Ch 10, dc in 4th ch from hook and in ea ch across.
Row 2: Ch 3, turn; skip first dc, dc in next 6 dc and in next ch.
Rep Row 2 until piece measures approximately 20" from beg ch.
Loops: Ch 8, do not turn; working across length of strip, (sl st, ch 8) twice around post of ea dc across, * turn, working across next column of dc, (sl st, ch 8) twice around post of ea st across; rep from * until all columns are complete, omitting last ch-8 at end of last st; fasten off, leaving a long end for sewing.

Projects were stitched with Jamie Pompadour: Peppermint Print #246.

FINISHING
Wrap a thin layer of polyester batting around ring. Cover batting with crocheted fabric, loop side out. Sew long seam on inside of ring; then sew short edges together.

Tie ribbon in a floppy bow and glue to top of wreath.

Glue baby trinkets to wreath as desired.

The nursery door is the ideal spot to hang this sweet wreath.

FRAME

MATERIALS
Sport-weight yarn,
   approximately:
1¾ oz. (195 yd.) variegated
Size G crochet hook
2 yd. ea ³⁄₁₆"-wide picot-edged
   ribbons: pink, blue, white
Various baby trinkets
Craft glue

FINISHED SIZE
To fit any frame desired

FIRST STRIP
Row 1: Ch 7, dc in 4th ch from
hook and in ea ch across.

Row 2: Ch 3, turn; skip first dc,
dc in next 3 dc and in next ch.

Rep Row 2 until piece measures
approximately 2" shorter than
bottom edge of frame.

Loops: Ch 8, do not turn; working across length of strip, (sl st,
ch 8) twice around post of ea st
across, * turn; working across
next column of dc, (sl st, ch 8)
twice around post of ea st across;
rep from * until all columns are
complete, omitting last ch-8 at
end of last st; fasten off.
Glue to bottom edge of frame.

REMAINING STRIPS
Work as for First Strip, until all
edges and/or divider bars of
frame are covered.

FINISHING
Tie ribbon in a floppy bow and
glue to corner of frame. Glue
baby trinkets to frame as desired.

Country Christmas

If you can't take your family to a mountain lodge to celebrate Christmas, bring the rustic coziness to them with this charming afghan and matching stocking. Hold two strands of yarn together when stitching the stocking to give it added bulkiness.

AFGHAN

MATERIALS

Sport-weight yarn, approximately:
25 oz. (2,175 yd.) beige, MC
15 oz. (1,305 yd.) brown, A
10 oz. (870 yd.) green, B
Size N crochet hook or size to obtain gauge
Yarn needle

FINISHED SIZE
Approximately 50" x 66"

Note: *Afghan is stitched holding 2 strands of yarn tog throughout.*

GAUGE
In patt, 5 sts and 5 rows = 2"

Note: *To change colors, work last yo of prev st with new color; fasten off old color. When instructed to work in sts 1 row below, work around ch-3 sps.*

With A, ch 120.
Row 1 (rs): Sc in 2nd ch from hook, dc in next 3 chs, * ch 3, skip next 3 chs, dc in next 3 chs; rep from * across to last ch, sc in last ch, change to MC.

Note: *Mark last row as rs.*
Row 2: Ch 1, turn; sc in first sc, * ch 3, skip next 3 dc **, dc in next 3 chs 1 row below; rep from * across, ending last rep at **, sc in last sc, change to B.
Row 3: Ch 1, turn; sc in first sc, dc in next 3 dc 1 row below, * ch 3, skip next 3 dc, dc in next 3 dc 1 row below; rep from * across to last sc, sc in last sc, change to A.
Row 4: Ch 1, turn; sc in first sc, * ch 3, skip next 3 dc **, dc in next 3 dc 1 row below; rep from * across, ending last rep at **, sc in last sc, change to MC.
Row 5: Rep Row 3, changing to B in last st.
Row 6: Rep Row 4, changing to A in last st.
Row 7: Rep Row 3, changing to MC in last st.
Row 8: Rep Row 4, changing to B in last st.
Rows 9–14: Rep Rows 3–8.
Row 15: Ch 1, turn; sc in first sc, dc in next 3 dc 1 row →

Projects were stitched with Wool-Ease Sportweight: Wheat #402, Mushroom #403, Green Heather #130.

below ch-3, * sc in next 3 dc, dc in next 3 dc 1 row below; rep from * across to last sc, sc in last sc.

Row 16: Ch 1, turn; sc in ea st across, change to MC.

Rows 17–34: Ch 1, turn; sc in ea sc across; at end of last row change to B.

Rows 35 and 36: Ch 1, turn; sc in ea sc across; at end of last row change to A.

Row 37: Ch 1, turn; sc in first sc, dc in next 3 sc, * ch 3, skip next 3 sc, dc in next 3 sc; rep from * across to last sc, sc in last sc, change to MC.

Row 38: Ch 1, turn; sc in first sc, * ch 3, skip next 3 dc **, dc in next 3 sc 1 row below; rep from * across, ending last rep at **, sc in last sc, change to B.

Rows 39–159: Rep Rows 3–38, 3 times; then rep Rows 3–15 once more.

BORDER

Rnd 1: Ch 1, do not turn; sc evenly around working 3 sc in ea corner; join with sl st to beg sc.

Rnds 2 and 3: Ch 1, sc in ea sc around working 3 sc in ea corner sc; join with sl st to beg sc; fasten off after last rnd.

TRIM

Foll *Chart*, holding 2 strands of yarn tog and centering patt, work in cross st, making 7 trees evenly sp across ea MC band.

Chart

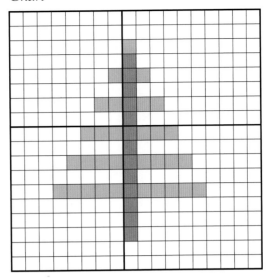

Chart Key

■ Brown, A
■ Green, B

Each Square on *Chart* represents one single crochet stitch.

*U*se a yarn that contains wool

to make this afghan extra

warm and cozy.

STOCKING

MATERIALS
Sport-weight yarn,
approximately:
5 oz. (435 yd.) beige, MC
5 oz. (435 yd.) brown, A
5 oz. (435 yd.) green, B
Size K crochet hook or size
to obtain gauge
Yarn needle

FINISHED SIZE
Approximately 7" x 16"

Note: Stocking is stitched holding 2 strands of yarn tog throughout. To change colors, work last yo of prev st with new color; fasten off old color.

GAUGE
In patt, 12 sts and 8 rows = 4"

PATTERN STITCHES
Double crochet dec (dc dec):
* Yo, insert hook in next st 1 row below and pull up lp, yo and draw through 2 lps; rep from * once more, yo and draw through all 3 lps on hook.
Single crochet dec (sc dec): Pull up a lp in ea of next first 2 sts or next 2 sts, yo and draw through all 3 lps on hook.

Note: When instructed to work in sts 1 row below, work around ch-sps.

STOCKING BODY
With A, ch 42.
Row 1 (rs): Sc in 2nd ch from hook, dc in next 3 chs, * ch 3,

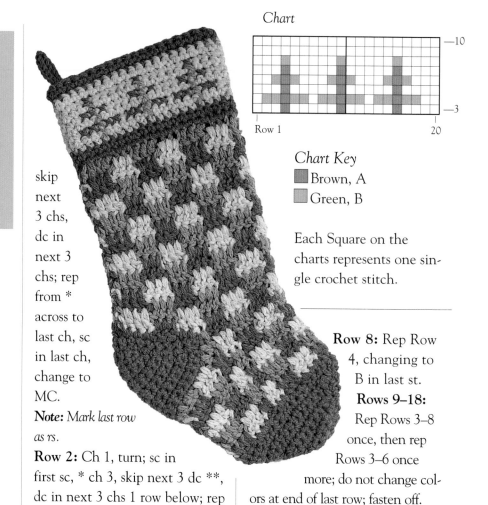

Chart

Chart Key
- Brown, A
- Green, B

Each Square on the charts represents one single crochet stitch.

skip next 3 chs, dc in next 3 chs; rep from * across to last ch, sc in last ch, change to MC.
Note: Mark last row as rs.
Row 2: Ch 1, turn; sc in first sc, * ch 3, skip next 3 dc **, dc in next 3 chs 1 row below; rep from * across, ending last rep at **, sc in last sc, change to B.
Row 3: Ch 1, turn; sc in first sc, dc in next 3 dc 1 row below, * ch 3, skip next 3 dc, dc in next 3 dc 1 row below; rep from * across to last sc, sc in last sc, change to A.
Row 4: Ch 1, turn; sc in first sc, * ch 3, skip next 3 dc **, dc in next 3 dc 1 row below; rep from * across, ending last rep at **, sc in last sc, change to MC.
Row 5: Rep Row 3, changing to B in last st.
Row 6: Rep Row 4, changing to A in last st.
Row 7: Rep Row 3, changing to MC in last st.

Row 8: Rep Row 4, changing to B in last st.
Rows 9–18: Rep Rows 3–8 once, then rep Rows 3–6 once more; do not change colors at end of last row; fasten off.

HEEL
Row 1 (rs): With rs facing, skip first 5 ch-3 sps and join B with sl st in center ch of next ch-3; ch 1, sc in dc 1 row below same ch and in next dc, sc in next 3 dc, sc in next 3 dc 1 row below, sc in last sc and in 1st sc of Row 18, sc in next 3 dc 1 row below, sc in next 3 dc, sc in next 2 dc 1 row below.
Row 2: Ch 1, turn; sc in first 12 sc.
Row 3: Ch 1, turn; sc in first 6 sc.
Row 4: Ch 1, turn; sc in first 6 sc and in next sc 2 rows below.
Rows 5–15: Ch 1, turn; sc in ea sc across and in next sc 3 rows below; fasten off after last row.

FOOT AND TOE

Row 1 (rs): With rs facing, skip first 9 sc of last row of heel and join A with sl st in next sc; ch 1, sc in same st as joining, dc in next 3 sc, ch 3, skip next 3 sc, dc in next 2 sc, dc in next skipped dc on Row 18 of stocking, * ch 3, skip next 3 dc **, dc in next 3 dc 1 row below; rep from * 2 times more, then rep from * to ** once, dc in next dc 1 row below and in first 2 sc on Row 15 of heel, ch 3, skip next 3 sc, dc in next 3 sc, sc in next sc, change to MC.

Row 2: Ch 1, turn; sc in first sc, ch 3, skip next 3 dc, dc in next 3 sc 1 row below, ch 3, skip next 3 dc, dc in next dc 1 row below, dc dec, * ch 3, skip next 3 dc **, dc in next 3 dc 1 row below; rep from * once more, then rep from * to ** once, dc dec, dc in next dc 1 row below, ch 3, skip next 3 dc, dc in next 3 sc 1 row below, ch 3, skip next 3 dc, sc in last sc, change to B.

Row 3: Ch 1, turn; sc in first sc, dc in next 3 dc 1 row below, ch 3, skip next 3 dc, dc in next dc 1 row below, dc dec, ch 2, skip next 2 sts, * dc in next 3 dc 1 row below **, ch 3, skip next 3 dc; rep from * once more, then rep from * to ** once, ch 2, skip next 2 sts, dc dec, dc in next dc 1 row below, ch 3, skip next 3 dc, dc in next 3 dc 1 row below, sc in last sc, change to A.

Row 4: Ch 1, turn; sc in first sc, ch 3, skip next 3 dc, dc in next 3 dc 1 row below, ch 2, skip next 2 sts, dc in next 2 sts 1 row below, * ch 3, skip next 3 dc **, dc in next 3 dc 1 row below; rep from

* once more, then rep from * to ** once, dc in next 2 sts 1 row below, ch 2, skip next 2 sts, dc in next 3 dc 1 row below, ch 3, skip next 3 dc, sc in last sc, change to MC.

Row 5: Ch 1, turn; sc in first sc, dc in next 3 dc 1 row below, ch 3, skip next 3 dc, dc in next 2 sts 1 row below, ch 2, skip next 2 dc, * dc in next 3 dc 1 row below **, ch 3, skip next 3 dc; rep from * 2 times more, then rep from * to ** once, ch 2, skip next 2 dc, dc in next 2 sts 1 row below, ch 3, skip next 3 dc, dc in next 3 dc 1 row below, sc in last sc, change to B.

Row 6: Rep Row 4, changing to A in last st.

Row 7: Rep Row 5, changing to MC in last st.

Row 8: Rep Row 4, changing to B in last st.

Row 9: Ch 1, turn; sc in first sc, dc in next 3 dc 1 row below, ch 3, skip next 3 dc, dc dec, ch 2, skip next 2 dc, * dc in next 3 dc 1 row below **, ch 3, skip next 3 dc; rep from * once, then rep from * to ** once more, ch 2, skip next 2 dc, dc dec, ch 3, skip next 3 dc, dc in next 3 dc 1 row below, sc in last sc; do not change colors.

Row 10: Ch 1, turn; sc dec, sc in next 2 dc and in next 3 dc 1 row below, sc in next st and in next 2 dc 1 row below, sc in next 3 dc and in next 2 dc 1 row below, pull up a lp in next dc 1 row below and in next dc, yo and draw through all 3 lps on hook, sc in next dc, pull up a lp in next dc and in next dc 1 row below, yo and draw through all 3 lps on hook, sc in

next 2 dc 1 row below and in next 3 dc, sc in next st and in next 3 dc 1 row below, sc in next 2 dc, sc dec.

Row 11: Ch 1, turn; * sc dec, sc in next 11 sc, sc dec **, sc in next sc; rep from * to ** once.

Row 12: Ch 1, turn; * sc dec, sc in next 9 sc, sc dec **, sc in next sc; rep from * to ** once.

Row 13: Ch 1, turn; * sc dec, sc in next 7 sc, sc dec **, sc in next sc; rep from * to ** once.

Row 14: Ch 1, turn; * sc dec, sc in next 5 sc, sc dec **, sc in next sc; rep from * to ** once.

Row 15: Ch 1, turn; * sc dec, sc in next 3 sc, sc dec **, sc in next sc; rep from * to ** once.

Row 16: Ch 1, turn; sc dec, * sc in next sc, sc dec; rep from * across; fasten off.

CUFF

Row 1 (rs): With rs facing and working across beg ch, join B with sl st in free lp of first ch; ch 1, sc in same st and in ea ch across.

Row 2: Ch 1, turn; sc in ea sc across, change to MC.

Rows 3–10: Ch 1, turn; sc in ea sc across; at end of last row change to B.

Rows 11 and 12: Ch 1, turn; sc in ea sc across.

Hanger: Ch 8; join with sl st in top of last sc made; fasten off.

FINISHING

Sew all seams together using corresponding colors.

Foll *Chart* and holding 2 strands of yarn tog, cross st 3 trees across one side of MC band.

Let It Snow!

These ornaments are ideal for making in multiples—one ball of yarn makes more than 45 snowflakes!

Hang them in a wreath or on a Christmas tree, or stitch them together to make a garland.

MATERIALS

(For each snowflake)
Sportweight yarn,
    approximately:
3½ yd. white
    (1 ball makes more than
    45 ornaments)
Size G crochet hook or size
    to obtain gauge
Fabric stiffener
Waxed paper

Use a yarn with an iridescent thread running through it to give your snowflakes added shimmer.

FINISHED SIZE

Approximately 2¾" in diameter

Ch 3, sl st in 1st ch to form a ring.

Rnd 1 (rs): Ch 1, 8 sc in ring; join with sl st in beg sc.

Rnd 2: Ch 5, (dc in next sc, ch 2) around; join with sl st in 3rd ch of beg ch-5.

Rnd 3: Ch 4, sl st in second ch from hook, ch 2, * sl st in next dc, ch 4, sl st in second ch from hook, ch 2; rep from * around; join with sl st in same st as beg ch-4; fasten off.

FINISHING

Immerse snowflake in stiffening solution. Lay snowflake on waxed paper with rs down; shape as desired. When dry, cut off loose ends.

Project was stitched with Wool-Ease: White/Multi #301.

'Tis the Season

My friends call me "Vanna Claus" around the holidays because they know how I love to surprise them with beautiful handmade afghans like this colorful Christmas throw.

FINISHED SIZE
Approximately 52" x 67"

GAUGE
In patt, 10 sc = 3"; 7 rows = 2"

Note: *To change colors, work last yo of prev st with new color; dropping prev color to ws of work. Do not carry yarn across row; fasten off color when no longer needed.*

With MC, ch 162 loosely.
Row 1 (ws): Reading *Chart*, pages 96–97, from left to right, sc in 2nd ch from hook and in next 4 chs, * change to A, sc in next ch, change to MC **, sc in next 14 chs; rep from * across, ending last rep at **, sc in last 5 chs.

Rows 2–221: Cont foll *Chart* as est, reading even (rs) rows from right to left and odd (ws) rows from left to right. Do not fasten off MC at end of last row.

BORDER
Rnd 1 (rs): Ch 1, turn; 3 sc in first sc, * work 157 sc evenly sp across to next corner, 3 sc in corner, work 217 sc evenly sp across end of rows to next corner **, 3 sc in corner; rep from * to ** once; join with sl st to beg sc.
Rnd 2: (Sl st, ch 1, sc) in next sc, * ch 5, skip next 4 sc, sc in next sc; rep from * around to last 4 sc, ch 1, skip last 4 sc, tr in beg sc to form last sp.
Rnd 3: Ch 1, sc around post of last tr made, (ch 5, sc in next ch-5 sp) around, ch 1, tr in beg sc to form last sp.
Rnd 4: Ch 1, sc around post of last tr made, * (7 dc, ch 2, 7 dc) in next corner ch-5 sp **, sc in next ch-5 sp, [(4 dc, ch 2, 4 dc) in next ch-5 sp, sc in next ch-5 sp] across to next corner ch-5 sp; rep from * 2 times more, then rep from * to ** once, [sc in next ch-5 sp, (4 dc, ch 2, 4 dc) in next ch-5 sp] across; join with sl st to bk lp only of beg sc.
Rnd 5: Ch 1, sc in bk lp only of same st as joining and in ea st across to next ch-2 sp, * (sc, ch 2, sc) in next ch-2 sp **, sc in bk lp only of ea st across to next ch-2 sp; rep from * around, ending last rep at **, sc in bk lp only of last 4 dc; join with sl st to both lps of beg sc; fasten off. ➜

Project was stitched with Wool-Ease: Cranberry #138, Fisherman #099, Forest Green Heather #180.

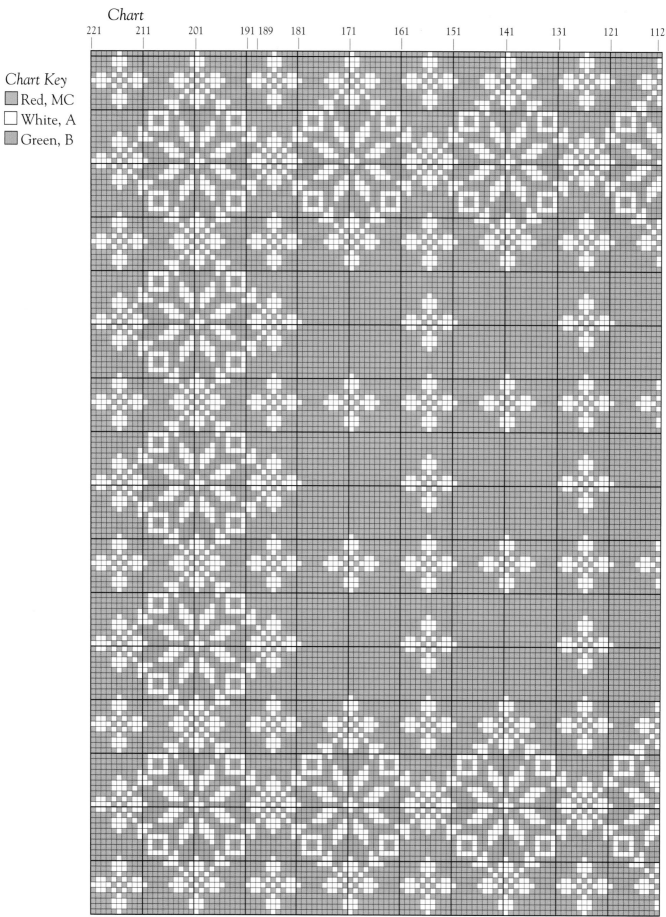

Chart Key
▨ Red, MC
☐ White, A
▨ Green, B

Each Square on *Chart* represents one single crochet stitch. Because the work is turned after each row, be sure to read all right side rows from right to left and all wrong side rows from left to right.

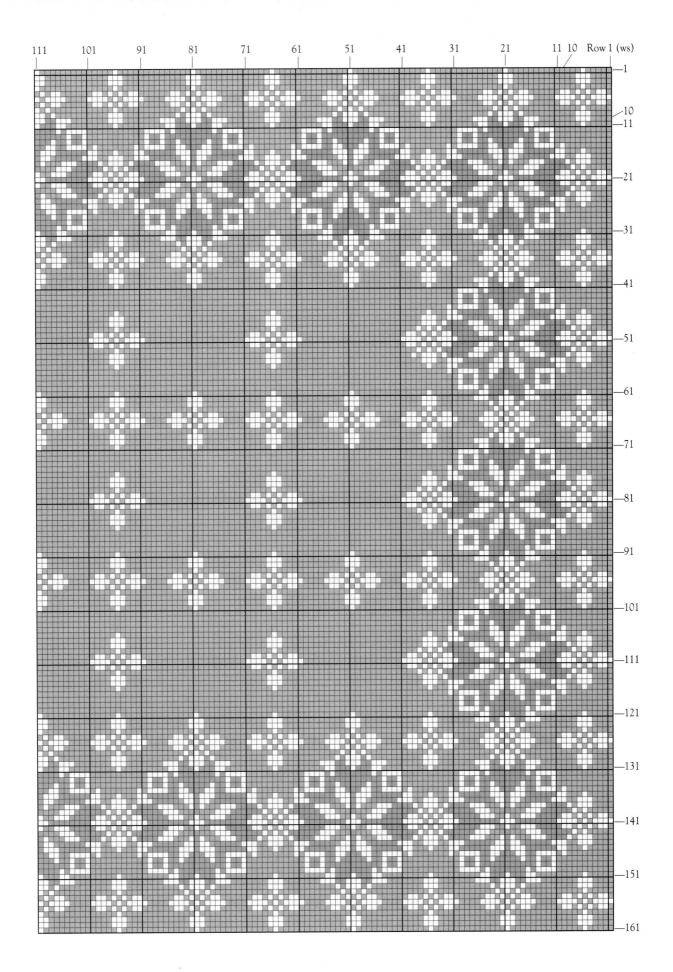

Holiday Dip Down

This festive throw begs youto curl up under it beside a flickering fire.

MATERIALS

Chunky-weight yarn, approximately:
15 oz. (680 yd.) green, MC
15 oz. (680 yd.) white, A
15 oz. (680 yd.) burgundy, B
Size K crochet hook or size to obtain gauge

FINISHED SIZE
Approximately 45" x 63"

GAUGE
In pat, 9 sts = 4"; 5 rows = 2¾"

PATTERN STITCH
Long sc (Lsc): Working around previous rnd(s), insert hook is sp before dc indicated, pull up a loop even with loop on hook, yo and draw through both loops on hook.

With MC, ch 94 loosely.
Row 1 (rs): Dc in 4th ch from hook and in ea ch across.
Note: *Mark last row as rs.*
Rows 2–4: Ch 3 [counts as first dc throughout], turn; dc in next dc and in each dc across, dc in top of tch; fasten off after last row.
Row 5: With rs facing, join A with sl st in first dc; ch 1, sc in same st as joining, Lsc in sp before next dc, * Lsc in sp before next dc 2 rows below, Lsc in sp before next dc 3 rows below, Lsc in sp before next dc 4 rows below, Lsc in sp before next dc 3 rows below, Lsc in sp before next dc 2 rows below, sc in sp before next dc; rep from * across.
Rows 6–9: Ch 3, turn; skip first st, dc in next st and in each st across; fasten off after last row.
Rows 10–14: With B, rep Rows 5–9.
Rows 15–19: With MC, rep Rows 5–9.
Rows 20–107: Rep Rows 5–19, 5 times; then rep Rows 5–17 once more; fasten off after last row.

BORDER
Rnd 1: With rs facing and working across last row, join B with sl st first dc; ch 3, 2 dc in same st as joining, dc in next dc and in ea dc across to last dc, 3 dc in last dc, dc evenly sp across end of rows to next corner, 3 dc in corner, dc in ea st across to next corner, 3 dc in corner, dc evenly sp across end of rows; join with sl st to top of beg ch 3.
Rnd 2: Ch 3, 3 dc in next dc, * dc in next dc and in ea dc across to center dc of next corner, 3 dc in center dc; rep from * 2 times more, dc in next dc and in ea dc across; join with sl st to top of beg ch-3; fasten off.
Rnd 3: With rs facing, join MC with sl st in any dc; ch 3, dc in next dc and in ea dc around working 3 dc in center dc of ea corner; join with sl st to top of beg ch-3; fasten off.
Rnd 4: With rs facing, join A with sl st in any dc; ch 1, sc in same st as joining and in ea dc around working 3 sc in center dc of ea corner; join with sl st to beg sc; fasten off.

Stitch this afghan in shades of blue and white, and it resembles rows of melting icicles.

Project was stitched with Jiffy: Forest Green #131, Fisherman #099, Wine #189.

Butterfly Blue Sweater

The basic design of this sweater is simple, but when you add the lacy neck, cuffs, and hem, then simple becomes spectacular!

MATERIALS
Chunky-weight yarn, approximately:
30 {36, 36, 42} oz. (925 {1,110; 1,110; 1,295} yd.) blue variegated
Size K crochet hook or size to obtain gauge
Yarn needle

Sizes: Sm, Med, Lg, X-Lg
Finished Measurements: 36", 40", 44", 48"

Size Note: Instructions are written for size Sm, with sizes Med, Lg, and X-Lg in braces { }. Instructions will be easier to read if you highlight all the numbers pertaining to your size. If only one number is given, it applies to all sizes.

GAUGE
In pat, 5 dc and 3 rows = 2"

PATTERN STITCH
Dec: * Yo, insert hook in next dc, yo and pull up a lp, yo and draw through 2 lps on hook; rep from * once more, yo and draw through all 3 lps on hook.

BACK
Ch 50 {54, 58, 62} loosely.

Row 1 (rs): Dc in 4th ch from hook and in ea ch across: 48 {52, 56, 60} sts.
Note: Mark last row as rs.
Row 2: Ch 3 [counts as first dc throughout], turn; skip first dc, dc in next dc and in ea dc across, dc in next ch.
Rep Row 2 until Back measures approximately 13" from beg ch.

Armhole Shaping
Row 1: Ch 1, turn; sl st in first 4 dc, ch 3, dc in next dc and in ea dc across to last 3 dc, leave last 3 dc unworked: 42 {46, 50, 54} dc.
Row 2: Ch 3, turn; skip first st, dc in next dc and in ea dc across.
Row 3: Ch 2, turn; skip first dc, dc in next dc [beg dec made], dc in next dc and in ea dc across to last 2 dc, dec: 40 {44, 48, 52} sts.
Rows 4–7 {4–7, 4–9, 4–9}: Rep Rows 2–3, 2 {2, 3, 3} times: 36 {40, 42, 46} sts.
Rep Row 2 until Back measures approximately 21" {21½", 22", 22½"} from beg ch.
Next Row: Ch 1, turn; sl st in first 3 dc, sc in next dc, hdc in next dc, dc in next dc and in ea dc across to last 5 dc, hdc in next dc, sc in next dc, sl st in last 3 dc; fasten off.

FRONT
Work as for Back until Front measures approximately 17" {17½", 18", 18½"}, ending by working a rs row.

Right Side
Row 1: Ch 3, turn; skip first dc, dc in next 12 {14, 14, 15} dc, dec, leave rem sts unworked: 14 {16, 16, 17} sts.
Row 2: Ch 2, turn; skip first st, dc in next dc and in ea dc across: 13 {15, 15, 16} dc.
Row 3: Ch 3, turn; skip first dc, dc in next dc and in ea dc across to last 2 dc, dec: 12 {14, 14, 15} sts.
Rows 4 and 5: Rep Rows 2–3: 10 {12, 12, 13} sts.
Row 6: Ch 3, turn; skip first st, dc in next dc and in ea dc across.
Row 7: Ch 1, turn; sl st in first 3 dc, sc in next dc, hdc in next dc, dc in next dc and in ea dc across; fasten off.

Left Side
Row 1: With ws facing, skip next 6 {6, 8, 10} dc from Right Side edge, join yarn with sl st in next dc; ch 2, dc in next dc and in ea dc across: 14 {16, 16, 17} dc. ➔

Row 2: Ch 3, turn; skip first dc, dc in next dc and in ea dc across to last 2 dc, dec: 13 {15, 15, 16} sts.

Row 3: Ch 2, turn; skip first st, dc in next dc and in ea dc across: 12 {14, 14, 15} dc.

Rows 4 and 5: Rep Rows 2–3: 10 {12, 12, 13} dc.

Row 6: Ch 3, turn; skip first dc, dc in next dc and in ea dc across.

Row 7: Ch 3, turn; skip first st, dc in next dc and in ea dc across to last 5 dc, hdc in next dc, sc in next dc, sl st in last 3 dc; fasten off.

SLEEVE (MAKE 2.)

Ch 24 {26, 28, 30} loosely.

Row 1 (rs): Dc in 4th ch from hook and in ea ch across: 22 {24, 26, 28} sts.

Note: Mark last row as rs.

Row 2: Ch 3, turn; dc in first dc and in ea dc across to last dc, 2 dc in last dc: 24 {26, 28, 30} dc.

Row 3: Ch 3, turn; skip first dc, dc in next dc and in ea dc across.

Rows 4–6: Rep Rows 2–3 once; then rep Row 2 once more: 28 {30, 32, 34} dc.

Rows 7 and 8: Ch 3, turn; skip first dc, dc in next dc and in ea dc across.

Row 9: Ch 3, turn; dc in first dc and in ea dc across to last dc, 2 dc in last dc: 30 {32, 34, 36} dc.

Rows 10–22: Rep Rows 7–9, 4 times; then rep Row 7 once more: 38 {40, 42, 44} dc.

Row 23: Ch 1, turn; sl st in first 4 dc, ch 3, dc in next dc and in ea dc across to last 3 dc, leave last 3 dc unworked: 32 {34, 36, 38} dc.

Rows 24–31 {24–32, 24–33, 24–34}: Ch 2, turn; skip first dc, dc in next dc and in ea dc across to last 2 dc, dec; fasten off after last row: 16 sts.

FINISHING

Sew shoulder seams. Sew Sleeves to body matching center of Sleeve to shoulder seam. Sew sleeve and side seams.

TRIM

Bottom

Rnd 1: With rs facing, join yarn with sl st in free lp of any ch; ch 4, 2 dc in same st, * skip next 2 chs, (2 dc, ch 1, 2 dc) in free lp of next ch; rep from * around to last 2 {1, 3, 2} ch(s), skip last 2 {1, 3, 2} ch(s), dc in same st as beg ch-4; join with sl st to 3rd ch of beg ch-4.

Rnds 2–4: (Sl st, ch 4, 2 dc) in first ch-1 sp, (2 dc, ch 1, 2 dc) in ea ch-1 sp around, dc in same sp as beg ch-4; join with sl st to 3rd ch of beg ch-4.

Rnd 5: (Sl st, ch 5, 2 dc) in first ch-1 sp, (2 dc, ch 2, 2 dc) in ea ch-1 sp around, dc in same sp as beg ch-5; join with sl st to 3rd ch of beg ch-5.

Rnd 6: (Sl st, ch 3, dc, ch 3, 2 dc) in first ch-2 sp, (2 dc, ch 3, 2 dc) in ea ch 2 sp around; join with sl st to first dc; fasten off.

Sleeve

Rnd 1: With rs facing, join yarn with sl st in free lp of any ch;

ch 4, 2 dc in same st as joining, * skip next 2 chs, (2 dc, ch 1, 2 dc) in free lp of next ch; rep from * around to last 3 {2, 1, 3} ch(s), skip last 3 {2, 1, 3} ch(s), dc in same st as beg ch-4; join with sl st to 3rd ch of beg ch-4.

Rnds 2–5: Rep Rnds 3–6 of Bottom trim.

Rep for 2nd sleeve.

Neck

Rnd 1: With rs facing, join yarn with sl st in first unworked dc on Back; ch 4, 2 dc in same st as joining, work (2 dc, ch 1, 2 dc) 3 {3, 3, 4} times evenly sp across Back, * work (2 dc, ch 1, 2 dc) 3 times evenly sp across end of rows **, work (2 dc, ch 1, 2 dc) 2 {2, 3, 4} times evenly sp across Front, rep from * to ** once, dc in same st as beg ch-4; join with sl st to 3rd ch of beg ch-4.

Rnds 2–5: Rep Rnds 3–6 of Bottom trim.

Project was stitched with Homespun: Windsor #341.

Bobble-Edged Slippers

These casual house shoes are a treat for the feet. You can easily adjust the stitches to accommodate any shape or size foot.

Sizes: Sm, Med, Lg
Sole Lengths: 7", 9", 11"

Size Note: *Instructions are written for size Sm, with sizes Med and Lg in braces { }. Instructions will be easier to read if you highlight all the numbers pertaining to your size. If only one number is given, it applies to all sizes.*

Note: *To change colors, work last yo of prev st with new color; drop unused color; do not fasten off.*

Zeros: To consolidate the length of this pattern, zeros are sometimes used so that all sizes can be combined. A zero indicates to do nothing until the next group of instructions.

GAUGE

In pat, 4 sc and 4 rows = 1"

PATTERN STITCHES

Dec: Pull up a lp in ea of first 2 sts or last 2 sts, yo and draw through all 3 lps on hook.

Popcorn: 4 Dc in st indicated, drop lp from hook, insert hook in first dc of 4 dc group, hook dropped lp and draw through.

SOLE

With CC, ch 4 {5, 6} loosely.

Row 1 (rs): 2 Sc in 2nd ch from hook, sc in next 1 {2, 3} ch(s), 2 sc in last ch: 5 {6, 7} sc.

Note: Mark last row as rs.

Row 2: Ch 1, turn; 2 sc in first sc, sc next 3 {4, 5} sc, 2 sc in last sc, change to MC: 7 {8, 9} sc.

Row 3: Ch 1, turn; 2 sc in first sc, sc in next 5 {6, 7} sc, 2 sc in last sc: 9 {10, 11} sc.

Row 4: Ch 1, turn; sc in ea sc across, change to dropped color.

Rows 5 and 6: Ch 1, turn; sc in ea sc across; change to dropped color in last sc on last row.

Rows 7 and 8: Rep Rows 5 and 6.

Rows 9–12 {9–18, 9–20}: Rep Rows 5–8, 1 {2, 3} time(s); then rep Rows 5–6, 0 {1, 0} time(s).

Row 13 {19, 21}: Ch 1, turn; 2 sc in first sc, sc in next sc and in ea sc across to last sc, 2 sc in last sc: 11 {12, 13} sc.

Row 14 {20, 22}: Ch 1, turn; sc in ea sc across, change to dropped color.

Row 15 {21, 23}: Ch 1, turn; sc in ea sc across.

Row 16 {22, 24}: Ch 1, turn; 2 sc in first sc, sc in next sc and in ea sc across to last sc, 2 sc in last sc, change to dropped color: 13 {14, 15} sc.

For Size Lg Only

Rows 25 and 26: Rep Rows 5–6.

Rows 27 and 28: Rep Rows 21–22: {17} sc.

For All Sizes

Rows 17–21 {23–29, 29–35}: Rep Rows 5–6, 2 {3, 3} times; then rep Row 5 once more.

Row 22 {30, 36}: Ch 1, turn; dec, sc in next sc and in ea sc across to last 2 sc, dec, change to dropped color: 11 {12, 15} sts.

Row 23 {31, 37}: Ch 1, turn; sc in ea st across.

Rows 24–26 {32–34, 38–42}: Rep Rows 22–23 {30–31, 36–37}, 1 {1, 2} time(s); then rep Row 22 {30, 36} once more: 7 {8, 9} sts.

Rows 27–28 {35–36, 43–44}: Ch 1, turn; dec, sc in next sc and in ea sc across to last 2 sc, dec; fasten off after last row: 3 {4, 5} sts.

INSTEP

With CC, ch 18 {22, 26} loosely.

Row 1 (rs): Sc in 2nd ch from hook and in ea ch across: 17 {21, 25} sc.

Row 2: Ch 1, turn; sc in ea sc across, change to MC.

Rows 3 and 4: Ch 1, turn; sc in ea sc across; change to dropped color in last st of last row.

For Size Lg Only

Rows 5 and 6: Rep Rows 3 and 4.

For All Sizes

Row 5 {5, 7}: Ch 1, turn; sc in ea sc across.

Row 6 {6, 8}: Ch 1, turn; dec, sc in next sc and in ea sc across to last 2 sc, dec, change to dropped color: 15 {19, 23} sts.

Rows 7–14 {7–16, 9–22}: Rep Rows 5–6 {5–6, 7–8} times: 7 {9, 9} sts.

Rows 15–16 {17–18, 23–24}: Ch 1, turn; dec, sc in next sc and in ea sc across to last 2 sc, →

dec; fasten off after last row: 3 {5, 5} sts.

Trim: With rs facing and working in free lps of beg ch, join MC with sl st in first ch; ch 1, sc in same st as joining, * Popcorn in next ch, sc in next ch; rep from * across; fasten off.

SIDES AND HEEL

With CC, ch 26 {38, 44} loosely.

Row 1 (rs): Sc in 2nd ch from hook and in ea ch across, change to MC: 25 {37, 43} sc.

Rows 2 and 3: Ch 1, turn; sc in ea sc across; change to dropped color in last sc on last row.

Rows 4–5 {4–7, 4–9}: Rep Rows 2 and 3, 1 {2, 3} times.

Last Row: With MC, ch 1, do not turn; working from left to right, sc in ea sc across [reverse sc]; fasten off.

FINISHING

Sew Sides and Heel to Instep.

ASSEMBLY

Rnd 1: Holding top of slipper to Sole, and working through both pieces, join MC with sl st in any st; ch 1, sc in evenly around; join with sl st to beg sc.

Rnd 2: Ch 1, do not turn; working from left to right, sc in ea sc around [reverse sc]; join with sl st to beg sc; fasten off.

Project was stitched with Wool-Ease: Fisherman #099, Grape Heather #144.

*G*ive *your busiest friend's feet some*

well-deserved pampering with

a pair of these snuggly slippers.

Finishing Touches

The woman who accessorizes with this matching chenille hat and purse will appear perfectly polished!
The style is playful enough for a teen but conservative enough for a mom or grandma.

HAT

MATERIALS

Worsted-weight yarn, approximately:
2.8 oz. (175 yd.) blue
Size H crochet hook or size to obtain gauge

Size: One size fits 21" to 23" head

GAUGE

Rnds 1 and 2 = 1½"

Ch 4; join with sl st to form a ring.

Rnd 1 (rs): Ch 1, 8 sc in ring; join with sl st to beg sc.

Rnd 2: Ch 1, 2 sc in ea sc around; join with sl st to beg sc.

Rnd 3: Ch 1, sc in same st as joining, 2 sc in next sc, (sc in next sc, 2 sc in next sc) around; join with sl st to beg sc.

Rnd 4: Ch 1, sc in same st as joining and in next sc, 2 sc in next sc, (sc in next 2 sc, 2 sc in next sc) around; join with sl st to beg sc.

Rnd 5: Ch 1, sc in same st as joining and in next 2 sc, 2 sc in next sc, (sc in next 3 sc, 2 sc in next sc) around; join with sl st to beg sc.

Rnd 6: Ch 1, sc in same st as joining and in next 3 sc, 2 sc in next sc, (sc in next 4 sc, 2 sc in next sc) around; join with sl st to beg sc.

Rnd 7: Ch 1, sc in same st as joining and in next 4 sc, 2 sc in next sc, (sc in next 5 sc, 2 sc in next sc) around; join with sl st to beg sc.

Rnd 8: Ch 1, sc in same st as joining and in next 5 sc, 2 sc in next sc, (sc in next 6 sc, 2 sc in next sc) around; join with sl st to beg sc.

Rnd 9: Ch 1, sc in same st as joining and in next 6 sc, 2 sc in next sc, (sc in next 7 sc, 2 sc in next sc) around; join with sl st to beg sc.

Rnd 10: Ch 1, sc in same st as joining and in next 7 sc, 2 sc in next sc, (sc in next 8 sc, 2 sc in next sc) around; join with sl st to beg sc.

Rnd 11: Ch 1, sc in same st as joining and in next 8 sc, 2 sc in next sc, (sc in next 9 sc, 2 sc in next sc) around; join with sl st to beg sc.

Rnd 12: Ch 1, working in bk lps only, 2 sc in same st as joining, sc in next 43 sc, 2 sc in next sc, sc in last 43 sc; join with sl st to both lps of beg sc.

Rnd 13: Ch 3, 2 dc in same st as joining, * skip next 2 sts, sc in next st, skip next 2 sts **, 5 dc in next st; rep from * around, ending last rep at **, 2 dc in same st as beg ch-3; join with sl st in top of beg ch-3.

Rnd 14: Ch 1, sc in same st as joining, * skip next 2 dc, 5 dc in next sc, skip next 2 dc **, sc in next dc; rep from * around, ending last rep at **; join with sl st to beg sc.

Rnds 15–21: Rep Rnds 13–14, 3 times; then rep Rnd 13 once more.

Rnd 22: Ch 1, sc in same st as joining and in ea st around; join with sl st to beg sc.

Rnd 23: Ch 1, sc in same st as joining and in next 8, 2 sc in next sc, (sc in next 9 sc, 2 sc in next sc) around; join with sl st to beg sc.

Rnd 24: Ch 1, sc in same st as joining and in next 9, 2 sc in next sc, (sc in next 10 sc, 2 sc in next sc) around; join with sl st to beg sc.

Rnd 25: Ch 1, sc in same st as joining and in next 25, 2 sc in next sc, (sc in next 26 sc, 2 sc in next sc) around; join with sl st to beg sc.

Rnd 26: Ch 1, sc in same st as joining and in next 26, 2 sc in next sc, (sc in next 27 sc, 2 sc in next sc) around; join with sl st to beg sc.

Rnd 27: Ch 1, sc in same st as joining and in next 27, 2 sc in next sc, (sc in next 28 sc, 2 sc in next sc) around; join with sl st to beg sc.

Rnd 28: Ch 1, sc in same st as joining and in ea sc around; join with sl st to beg sc; fasten off. ➜

Project was stitched with Chenille Sensations: Midnight Blue #110.

PURSE

MATERIALS

Worsted-weight yarn, approximately:
2.8 oz. (175 yd.) blue
Size H crochet hook or size to obtain gauge

Size: Approximately 9" x 8"

GAUGE
Rnds 1–4 = 8" x 2¼"

Ch 25 loosely.

Rnd 1: 2 Sc in 2nd ch from hook, sc in ea ch across to last ch, 3 sc in last ch, sc in free lp of ea ch across; join with sl st to beg sc.

Rnd 2: Ch 1, 2 sc in same st as joining and in next sc, sc in next 22 sc, 2 sc in ea of next 3 sc, sc in next 22 sc, 2 sc in last sc; join with sl st to beg sc.

Rnd 3: Ch 1, sc in same st as joining, (2 sc in next sc, sc in next sc) twice, sc in next 22 sc, (2 sc in next sc, sc in next sc) 3 times, sc in next 22 sc, 2 sc in last sc; join with sl st to beg sc.

Rnd 4: Ch 1, sc in same st as joining, 2 sc in next sc, sc in next 2 sc, 2 sc in next sc, sc in next 24 sc, 2 sc in next sc, (sc in next 2 sc, 2 sc in next sc) twice, sc in next 24 sc, 2 sc in next sc, sc in last sc; join with sl st to beg sc.

Rnd 5: Ch 1, working in bk lps only, sc in same st as joining and in next 3 sc, * 2 sc in next sc, sc in next 28 sc, 2 sc in next sc **, sc in next 4 sc; rep from * to ** once; join with sl st to both lps of beg sc.

Rnd 6: Ch 3, 2 dc in same st as joining, * skip next 2 sts, sc in next st, skip next 2 sts **, 5 dc in next st; rep from * around, ending last rep at **, 2 dc in same st as beg ch-3; join with sl st to top of beg ch-3.

Rnd 7: Ch 1, sc in same st as joining, * skip next 2 dc, 5 dc in next sc, skip next 2 dc **, sc in next dc; rep from * around, ending last rep at **; join with sl st to beg sc.

Rnds 8–17: Rep Rnds 6–7, 5 times.

Rnds 18–20: Ch 1, sc in same st as joining and in ea st around; join with sl st to beg sc.

Rnd 21: Ch 1, sc in same st as joining and in next 56 sc, ch 12, sc in last 15 sc; join with sl st to beg sc; fasten off.

FINISHING

Handle (Make 2.)
Ch 42.

Foundation (rs): 2 Sc in 2nd ch from hook, sc in ea ch across to last ch, 3 sc in last ch, sc in free lp of ea ch across; join with sl st to beg sc.

Row 1: Sl st in next sc, ch 1, sc in same st and in next 40 sc; fasten off.

Sew handles to inside top edge of sc rnds.

Button
Ch 4; join with sl st to form a ring.

Rnd 1: Ch 3, 12 dc in ring; join with sl st to top of beg ch-3; fasten off.

Sew button on rs of front opposite closure lp.

Project was stitched with Chenille Sensations: Midnight Blue #110.

Everything's Rosy Twinset

A twinset is a fashion classic that looks good on every woman. Stitch the set in the recipient's favorite color. The yarn used for this project comes in a wide range of shades, so you are bound to find one she'll love.

CARDIGAN

MATERIALS
Worsted-weight yarn,
approximately:
18 {21, 21, 24} oz. (1,180
  {1,380; 1,380; 1,575} yd.)
  rose
⅝" buttons: 6 {6, 7, 7}
Size H crochet hook or size
  to obtain gauge
Yarn needle

Sizes: Sm, Med, Lg, X-Lg
Finished Measurements: 42",
45", 48", 52"

*Size Note: Instructions are written
for size Sm, with sizes Med, Lg,
and X-Lg in braces { }. Instructions
will be easier to read if you highlight
all the numbers pertaining to your
size. If only one number is given, it
applies to all sizes.*

GAUGE
In pat, 13 hdc and 12 rows = 4"

PATTERN STITCH
Cluster: * Yo twice, insert hook
in sc indicated, yo and pull up a
lp, (yo and draw through 2 lps
on hook) twice; rep from * 3
times more, yo and draw through
all 5 lps on hook.

BACK
Ch 69 {75, 79, 85} loosely.
Row 1 (rs): Sc in 2nd ch from
hook and in ea ch across: 68 {74,
78, 84} sc.
Note: Mark last row as rs.
Row 2: Ch 1, turn; hdc in ea st
across.
Rep Row 2 until Back measures
approximately 12" {13", 13¾",
13¾"} from beg ch.

Armhole Shaping
Row 1: Ch 1, turn; skip first hdc,
sl st in next 4 {4, 5, 5} hdc, sc in
next hdc, hdc in next hdc and in
ea hdc across to last 6 {6, 7, 7}
hdc, sc in next hdc, leave rem sts
unworked: 58 {64, 66, 72} sts.
Rows 2–3 {2–3, 2–4, 2–4}: Ch
1, turn; skip first sc, sc in next
hdc, hdc in next hdc and in ea
hdc across to last 2 sts, sc in next
hdc, leave last sc unworked: 54
{60, 60, 66} sts.
Row 4 {4, 5, 5}: Ch 1, turn; hdc
in ea st across.
Row 5 {5, 6, 6}: Ch 1, turn;
skip first hdc, sc in next hdc, hdc
in next hdc and in ea hdc across
to last 2 hdc, sc in next hdc,
leave last hdc unworked: 52 {58,
58, 62} sts.
Row 6 {6, 7, 7}: Ch 1, turn; hdc
in ea st across.
*For Sizes Med, Lg, and X-Lg
Only*
Row 7, 8, 8: Rep Row {5, 6, 6}:
{56, 56, 60} sts.
For All Sizes
Rows 7–9 {8–10, 9–11, 9–11}:
Rep Row 6 {6, 7, 7}.
Row 10 {11, 12, 12}: Rep Row
5 {5, 6, 6}: 50 {54, 54, 58} sts.
Rep Row 6 {6, 7, 7} until Back
measures approximately 21" {22",
23", 23"} from beg ch, ending by
working a ws row.
Next Row: Ch 1, turn; skip first
hdc, sl st in next 2 hdc, sc in
next hdc, hdc in next hdc and in
ea hdc across to last 4 hdc, sc in
next hdc, leave remaining sts
unworked: 44 {48, 48, 52} sts.

Neck and Shoulder Shaping

Left Side
Row 1: Ch 1, turn; skip first sc,
sl st in next 5 {6, 6, 6} hdc, sc in
next hdc, hdc in next 7 {8, 8, 8}
hdc, leave remaining sts
unworked.
Row 2: Ch 1, turn; hdc in first
5 {6, 6, 6} hdc, sc in next hdc,
leave rem sts unworked; fasten off.

Right Side
Row 1: With ws facing, skip
next 16 {18, 18, 20} sts from Left
Side edge, join yarn with sl st in
next hdc; ch 1, hdc in same st as
joining and in next 6 {7, 7, 7}
hdc, sc in next hdc, leave rem sts
unworked.
Row 2: Ch 1, turn; skip first sc, sl
st in next hdc, sc in next hdc, hdc
last in 5 {6, 6, 6} hdc; fasten off.

RIGHT FRONT
Ch 34 {37, 39, 42} loosely.
Row 1 (rs): Sc in 2nd ch from
hook and in ea ch across: 33 {36,
38, 41} sc.
Note: Mark last row as rs.
Row 2: Ch 1, turn; hdc in ea st
across.
Rep Row 2 until Back measures
approximately 12" {13", 13¾",
13¾"} from beg ch, ending by
working a ws row.

Armhole Shaping

Row 1: Ch 1, turn; hdc in ea hdc across to last 6 {6, 7, 7} hdc, sc in next hdc, leave rem sts unworked: 28 {31, 32, 35} sts.

Row 2: Ch 1, turn; skip first sc, sc in next hdc, hdc in next hdc and in ea hdc across: 27 {30, 31, 34} sts.

Row 3: Ch 1, turn; hdc in ea hdc across to last 2 sts, sc in next hdc, leave last sc unworked: 26 {29, 30, 33} sts.

For Sizes Sm and Med Only

Row 4: Ch 1, turn; hdc in ea st across.

Row 5: Ch 1, turn; hdc in ea hdc across to last 2 sts, sc in next hdc, leave last st unworked: 25 {28} sts.

For Size Sm Only

Rows 6–9: Rep Row 4.

Row 10: Ch 1, turn; skip first hdc, sc in next hdc, hdc in next hdc and in ea hdc across; do not fasten off: 24 sts.

For Size Med Only

Rows 6–10: Rep Rows 4–5 once; then rep Row 4, 3 times: {27} sts.

Row 11: Rep Row 5; do not fasten off: {26} sts.

For Sizes Lg and X-Lg Only

Row 4: Ch 1, turn; skip first st, sc in next hdc, hdc in next hdc and in ea hdc across: {29, 32} sts.

Row 5: Ch 1, turn; hdc in ea st across.

Rows 6–8: Rep Rows 4–5 once; then rep Row 4 once more: {27, 30} sts.

Rows 9–11: Rep Row 5.

Row 12: Rep Row 4: {26, 29} sts.

For All Sizes

Row 11 {12, 13, 13}: Ch 1, turn; hdc in ea st across.

Rep Row 11 {12, 13, 13} until Front measures approximately 18½" {19½", 20½", 20½"} from beg ch, ending by working a rs row.

Neck and Shoulder Shaping

Row 1: Ch 1, turn; hdc in ea hdc across to last 3 {3, 3, 4} hdc, leave rem sts unworked: 21 {23, 23, 25} sts.

Row 2: Ch 1, turn; skip first st, hdc in next hdc and in ea hdc across: 20 {22, 22, 24} sts.

Row 3: Ch 1, turn; hdc in ea hdc across to last 2 sts, sc in next hdc, leave last st unworked: 19 {21, 21, 23} sts.

Rows 4–5 {4–5, 4–5, 4–7}: Rep Rows 2 and 3, 1 {1, 1, 2} time(s): 17 {19, 19, 19} sts.

Row 6 {6, 6, 8}: Ch 1, turn; hdc in ea st across.

Rep Row 6 {6, 6, 8} until Right Front measures approximately 21" {22", 23", 23"} from beg ch, ending by working a ws row.

Next Row: Ch 1, turn; hdc in ea hdc across to last 4 hdc, sc in next hdc, leave rem sts unworked.

Next Row: Ch 1, turn; skip first sc, sl st in next 5 {6, 6, 6} hdc, sc in next hdc, hdc in last 7 {8, 8, 8} hdc.

Last Row: Ch 1, turn; hdc in first 5 {6, 6, 6} hdc, sc in next hdc, leave rem sts unworked; fasten off.

Buttonhole Band

Row 1: With rs facing, join yarn with sl st in end of Row 1; ch 1, work 60 {63, 66, 66} sc evenly sp across to next corner.

Row 2: Ch 1, turn; sc in ea sc across.

Row 3 [buttonhole row]: Ch 1, turn; sc in first 3 {4, 3, 3} sc, * ch 1, skip next sc, sc in next 10 {10, 9, 9} sc; rep from * 4 {4, 5, 5} times, ch 1, skip next sc, sc in last 2 {3, 2, 2} sc.

Row 4: Ch 1, turn; sc in ea sc and in ea ch-1 sp across.

Row 5: Ch 1, turn; sc in ea sc across; fasten off.

LEFT FRONT

Ch 34 {37, 39, 42} loosely.

Row 1 (rs): Sc in 2nd ch from hook and in ea ch across: 33 {36, 38, 41} sc.

Note: *Mark last row as rs.*

Row 2: Ch 1, turn; hdc in ea st across.

Rep Row 2 until Back measures approximately 12" {13", 13¼", 13¾"} from beg ch, ending by working a ws row.

Armhole Shaping

Work as for Right Front until Left Front measures approximately 18½" {19½", 20½", 20½"} from beg ch, ending by working a ws row.

Neck and Shoulder Shaping

Work as for Right Front until Left Front measures approximately 21" {22", 23", 23"} from beg ch, ending by working a ws row. ➔

Next Row: Ch 1, turn; skip first hdc, sl st in next 2 hdc, sc in next hdc, hdc in next hdc and in ea hdc across.

Next Row: Ch 1, turn; hdc in next 7 {8, 8, 8} hdc, sc in next hdc, leave rem sts unworked.

Last Row: Ch 1, turn; skip first sc, sl st in next hdc, sc in next hdc, hdc in last 5 {6, 6, 6} hdc; fasten off.

Button Band

Row 1: With rs facing, join yarn with sl st at left front neck edge; ch 1, work 60 {63, 66, 66} sc evenly sp across to next corner.

Rows 2–4: Ch 1, turn; sc in ea sc across; fasten off after last row.

SLEEVE (MAKE 2.)

Ch 26 {28, 32, 34} loosely.

Row 1 (rs): Sc in 2nd ch from hook and in ea ch across: 25 {27, 31, 33} sc.

Row 2: Ch 1, turn; hdc in ea st across.

Row 3: Ch 1, turn; 2 hdc in first hdc, hdc in next hdc and in ea hdc across to last hdc, 2 hdc in last hdc: 27 {29, 33, 35} hdc.

Rows 4–6: Ch 1, turn; hdc in ea st across.

Rows 7–15: Rep Rows 3–6, twice; then rep Row 3 once more: 33 {35, 39, 41} hdc.

Rows 16 and 17: Ch 1, turn; hdc in ea st across.

Row 18: Ch 1, turn; 2 hdc in first hdc, hdc in next hdc and in ea hdc across to last hdc, 2 hdc in last hdc: 35 {37, 41, 43} hdc.

Rows 19–39: Rep Rows 16–18,

7 times: 49 {51, 55, 57} hdc.

Rows 40–45 {40–47, 40–49, 40–51}: Rep Row 2.

Sleeve Cap

Row 1: Ch 1, turn; skip first hdc, sl st in next 2 hdc, sc in next hdc, hdc in next hdc and in ea hdc across to last 4 hdc, sc in next hdc, leave rem sts unworked: 43 {45, 49, 51} sts.

Row 2: Ch 1, turn; skip first st, sl st in next hdc, sc in next hdc, hdc in next hdc and in ea hdc across to last 3 sts, sc in next hdc, leave rem sts unworked: 39 {41, 45, 47} sts.

Rows 3–5: Ch 1, turn; skip first sc, sc in next hdc, hdc in next hdc and in ea hdc across to last 2 sts, sc in next hdc, leave last st unworked: 33 {35, 39, 41} sts.

Row 6: Ch 1, turn; hdc in ea st across.

Row 7: Ch 1, turn; skip first sc, sc in next hdc, hdc in next hdc and in ea hdc across to last 2 sts, sc in next hdc, leave last st unworked: 31 {33, 37, 39} sts.

Row 8: Rep Row 6.

Rows 9 and 10: Rep Rows 3–4: 27 {29, 33, 35} sts.

Rows 11–16: Rep Rows 6 and 7, 3 times: 21 {23, 27, 29} sts.

Rows 17–20 {17–23, 17–23, 17–23}: (Rep Row 6, rep Row 7 twice) 1 {2, 2, 2} times: 17 {15, 19, 21} sts.

Sizes Sm and Med Only

Fasten off.

Sizes Lg and X-Lg Only

Rows 24–25: Rep Row 7; fasten off after last row: {15, 17} sts.

FINISHING

Sew shoulder seams. Sew Sleeves to body matching center of Sleeve to shoulder seam. Sew sleeve and side seams. Sew buttons to button band opposite buttonholes.

Collar

Ch 70 {70, 74, 86}.

Row 1: Sc in 2nd ch from hook and in ea ch across.

Row 2 (rs): Ch 1, turn; sc in first sc, * ch 4, skip next sc, Cluster in next sc, ch 4, skip next sc, sc in next sc; rep from * across; do not fasten off.

Joining: Pin ws of Collar to rs of cardigan along neck opening, working through both pieces, sc evenly across to next corner; do not fasten off.

Body Trim: Ch 1, do not turn; sc in ea sc across button band to last sc, (sc, ch 1, sc) in last sc; working across bottom edge, * ch 4, skip next st, Cluster in next st, ch 4, skip next st, sc in next st; rep from * across to next corner; join with sl st to first sc on last row of buttonhole band; fasten off.

Sleeve Trim: With rs facing, join yarn with sl st in seam; ch 1, sc in same st as joining, * ch 4, skip next ch **, Cluster in next ch, ch 4, skip next ch, sc in next ch; rep from * around, ending last rep at **; join with sl st to beg sc; fasten off.

Rep for 2nd Sleeve.

SHELL

MATERIALS

Worsted-weight yarn, approximately:
15 {15, 18, 18} oz. (985 {985; 1,180; 1,180} yd.) rose
Size H crochet hook or size to obtain gauge
Yarn needle

Sizes: Sm, Med, Lg, X-Lg
Finished Measurements: 36", 40", 44", 48"

Size Note: Instructions are written for size Sm, with sizes Med, Lg, and X-Lg in braces { }. Instructions will be easier to read if you highlight all the numbers pertaining to your size. If only one number is given, it applies to all sizes.

GAUGE

In pat, 13 hdc and 12 rows = 4"

BACK

Ch 63 {67, 73, 79} loosely.
Row 1 (rs): Sc in 2nd ch from hook and in ea ch across: 62 {66, 72, 78} sc.
Note: Mark last row as rs.
Row 2: Ch 1, turn; hdc in ea st across.
Rep Row 2 until Back measures approximately 12¼" {13¼", 14", 14"} from beg ch.

Armhole Shaping

Row 1: Ch 1, turn; skip first hdc, sl st in next 3 {3, 4, 5} hdc, sc in next hdc, hdc in next hdc and in ea hdc across to last 5 {5, 6, 7} hdc, sc in next hdc, leave rem sts unworked: 54 {58, 62, 66} sts.
Rows 2–3 {2–3, 2–4, 2–4}: Ch 1, turn; skip first sc, sc in next hdc, hdc in next hdc and in ea hdc across to last 2 sts, sc in next hdc, leave last sc unworked: 50 {54, 56, 60} sts.
Row 4 {4, 5, 5}: Ch 1, turn; hdc in ea st across.
Row 5 {5, 6, 6}: Ch 1, turn; skip first hdc, sc in next hdc, hdc in next hdc and in ea hdc across to last 2 hdc, sc in next hdc, leave last hdc unworked: 48 {52, 54, 58} sts.
Row 6 {6, 7, 7}: Ch 1, turn; hdc in ea st across.

For Sizes Med, Lg, and X-Lg Only

Row 7, 8, 8: Rep Row {5, 6, 6}: {50, 52, 56} sts.

For All Sizes

Rows 7–9 {8–10, 9–11, 9–11}: Rep Row 6 {6, 7, 7} twice.
Row 10 {11, 12, 12}: Rep Row 5 {5, 6, 6}: 46 {48, 50, 54} sts.
Rep Row 6 {6, 7, 7} until Back measures approximately 20½" {21½", 22½", 22½"} from beg ch, ending by working a ws row.
Next Row: Ch 1, turn; skip first hdc, sl st in next 4 hdc, sc in next hdc, hdc in next hdc and in ea hdc across to last 5 hdc, sc in next hdc, leave rem sts unworked: 36 {38, 40, 44} sts.

Neck and Shoulder Shaping
Left Side

Row 1: Ch 1, turn; skip first sc, sl st in next 3 hdc, sc in next hdc, hdc in next 6 {6, 7, 8} hdc, leave remaining sts unworked.
Row 2: Ch 1, turn; hdc in first 4 {4, 5, 6} hdc, sc in next hdc, leave rem sts unworked; fasten off.

Right Side

Row 1: With ws facing, skip next 14 {16, 16, 18} sts from Left Side edge, join yarn with sl st in next hdc; ch 1, hdc in same st as joining and in next 5 {5, 6, 7} hdc, sc in next hdc, leave rem sts unworked.
Row 2: Ch 1, turn; skip first sc, sl st in next hdc, sc in next hdc, hdc last in 4 {4, 5, 6} hdc; fasten off.

FRONT

Work as for Back until Front measures approximately 19" {19½", 20", 20"} from beg ch, ending by working a rs row: 46 {48, 50, 54} sts.

Neck and Shoulder Shaping

Right Side

Row 1: Ch 1, turn; hdc in first 19 {20, 20, 21} hdc, sc in next hdc, leave rem sts unworked.
Row 2: Ch 1, turn; skip first st, hdc in next hdc and in ea hdc across. ➔

Projects were stitched with Wool-Ease: Dark Rose Heather #139.

Row 3: Ch 1, turn; hdc in ea hdc across to last hdc, leave last hdc unworked.

Rows 4 and 5: Rep Rows 2 and 3.

For Sizes Med, Lg, and X-Lg Only

Rows 6–7, 6–9, 6–9: Ch 1, turn; hdc in ea hdc across.

For All Sizes

Row 6 {8, 10, 10}: Ch 1, turn; hdc in ea hdc across to last 6 hdc, sc in next hdc, leave rem sts unworked.

Row 7 {9, 11, 11}: Ch 1, turn; skip first sc, sl st in next 3 hdc, sc in next hdc, hdc in last 6 {6, 7, 8} hdc.

Row 8 {10, 12, 12}: Ch 1, turn; hdc in first 4 {4, 5, 6} hdc, sc in next hdc, leave rem sts unworked; fasten off.

Left Side

Row 1: With ws facing, skip next 6 {6, 8, 10} sts from Right Side edge, join yarn with sl st in next hdc; ch 1, sc in same st as joining, hdc in next hdc and in ea hdc across.

Row 2: Ch 1, turn; hdc in ea hdc across to last st, leave last st unworked.

Row 3: Ch 1, turn; skip first st, hdc in next hdc and in ea hdc across.

Rows 4 and 5: Rep Rows 2 and 3.

For Sizes Med, Lg, and X-Lg Only

Rows 6–7, 6–9, 6–9: Ch 1, turn; hdc in ea hdc across.

For All Sizes

Row 6 {8, 10, 10}: Ch 1, turn; skip first hdc, sl st in next 4 hdc, sc in next hdc, hdc in next hdc and in ea hdc across.

Row 7 {9, 11, 11}: Ch 1, turn; hdc in first 6 {6, 7, 8} hdc, sc in next hdc, leave rem sts unworked.

Row 8 {10, 12, 12}: Ch 1, turn; skip first sc, sl st in next hdc, sc in next hdc, hdc in last 4 {4, 5, 6} hdc; fasten off.

SLEEVE (MAKE 2.)

Ch 43 {47, 51, 55} loosely.

Row 1 (rs): Sc in 2nd ch from hook and in ea ch across: 42 {46, 50, 54} hdc.

Rows 2 and 3: Ch 1, turn; hdc in ea st across.

Row 4: Ch 1, turn; 2 hdc in first hdc, hdc in next hdc and in ea hdc across to last hdc, 2 hdc in last hdc: 44 {48, 52, 56} hdc.

Rows 5–11: Ch 1, turn; hdc in ea hdc across.

Sleeve Cap

Row 1: Ch 1, turn; skip first hdc, sl st in next 2 hdc, sc in next hdc, hdc in next hdc and in ea hdc across to last 4 hdc, sc in next hdc, leave rem sts unworked: 36 {42, 46, 50} sts.

Row 2: Ch 1, turn; skip first st, sl st in next hdc, sc in next hdc, hdc in next hdc and in ea hdc across to last 3 sts, sc in next hdc, leave rem sts unworked: 32 {36, 40, 44} sts.

Rows 3–5: Ch 1, turn; skip first sc, sc in next hdc, hdc in next hdc and in ea hdc across to last 2 sts, sc in next hdc, leave last st unworked: 26 {30, 34, 38} sts.

Row 6: Ch 1, turn; hdc in ea st across.

Row 7: Ch 1, turn; skip first sc, sc in next hdc, hdc in next hdc and in ea hdc across to last 2 sts, sc in next hdc, leave last st unworked: 24 {28, 32, 36} sts.

Row 8: Rep Row 6.

Rows 9 and 10: Rep Rows 3 and 4: 20 {24, 28, 32} sts.

Rows 11–14: Rep Rows 6 and 7, twice: 16 {20, 24, 28} sts.

Rows 15–17 {15–20, 15–20, 15–20}: (Rep Row 6, rep Row 7 twice) 1 {2, 2, 2} times: 12 {12, 16, 20} sts.

Sizes Sm and Med Only

Fasten off.

Sizes Lg and X-Lg Only

Rows 21–22, 21–23: Rep Row 7 {2, 3} times; fasten off after last row: {12, 14} sts.

FINISHING

Sew shoulder seams. Sew Sleeves to body matching center of Sleeve to shoulder seam. Sew sleeve and side seams.

Neck Trim: With rs facing, join yarn with sl st in any st; ch 1, sc evenly around neck opening; join with sl st to beg sc; fasten off.

Play-with-Me Plaid Sweater

This charming sweater would look equally cute on a girl or a boy. Sports enthusiasts may want to stitch it and the matching afghan on page 73 in their favorite team colors. Carry it to the big game to keep little fans warm.

MATERIALS

Sportweight yarn,
approximately:
15 {17½, 20, 20} oz. (1,010
{1,175; 1,345; 1,345} yd.)
white, MC
5 oz. (335 yd.) yellow, A
2½ oz. (170 yd.) lilac, B
2½ oz. (170 yd.) green, C
Sizes F and G crochet
hooks or sizes to obtain
gauge
Yarn needle

Sizes: Sm, Med, Lg, X-Lg
Finished Measurements: 27",
29", 31", 32"

Size Note: Instructions are written for size Sm, with sizes Med, Lg, and X-Lg in braces { }. Instructions will be easier to read if you highlight all the numbers pertaining to your size. If only one number is given, it applies to all sizes.

GAUGE

In pat, 9 sts and 9 rows= 2"

PATTERN STITCH

Dec: Pull up a lp in ea of first 2 sc or last 2 sc, yo and draw though all 3 lps on hook.

BACK

Ribbing

With smaller hook and MC, ch 7 {9, 11, 11} loosely.
Row 1: Sc in 2nd ch from hook and in ea ch across.
Row 2: Ch 1, turn; sc in bk lp only of ea sc across.
Rep Row 2 until ribbing measures approximately 12" {13", 14", 15"} slightly stretched.

Body

Change to larger hook.
Row 1 (rs): Ch 1, do not turn; work 63 {67, 69, 73} sc evenly sp across end of rows.
Note: Mark last row as rs.
Rows 2–66 {2–69, 2–75, 2–81}: Ch 1, turn; sc in both lps of ea sc across; fasten off after last row.

FRONT

Work as for Back through Row 55 {57, 63, 67}; do not fasten off.
Right Neck Shaping
Row 1: Ch 1, turn; sc in first 25 {26, 26, 27} sc, leave rem sts unworked.
Row 2: Ch 1, turn; dec, sc in next sc and in ea sc across.
Row 3: Ch 1, turn; sc in ea st across.
Rows 4–10: Rep Rows 2 and 3, 3 times; then rep Row 2 once more.
Last 1 {2, 2, 4} Row(s): Ch 1, turn; sc in ea st across; fasten off after last row.
Left Neck Shaping
Row 1: With ws facing, skip next 13 {15, 17, 19} sc from Right Neck edge, join MC with sl st in next sc; ch 1, sc in

K̶eep your little one

looking good and feeling warm with

this special gift.

⤜✥⤐

Project was stitched with Microspun: Lily White #100, Buttercup #158, Lime #194, Lilac #144.

same st as joining and in ea sc across.

Row 2: Ch 1, turn; sc in ea sc across to last 2 sc, dec.

Row 3: Ch 1, turn; sc in ea sc across.

Rows 4–10: Rep Rows 2–3, 3 times; then rep Row 2 once more.

Last 1 {2, 2, 4} Row(s): Ch 1, turn; sc in ea st across; fasten off after last row.

SLEEVE (MAKE 2.)

Ribbing

With smaller hook and MC, ch 7 {9, 11, 11} loosely.

Row 1: Sc in 2nd ch from hook and in ea ch across.

Row 2: Sc in bk lp only of ea sc across.

Rep Row 2 until ribbing measures approximately 6" {6½", 7", 7"} slightly stretched.

Body

Change to larger hook.

Row 1: Ch 1, do not turn; work 31 {33, 35, 35} sc evenly sp across end of rows.

Row 2: Ch 1, turn; 2 sc in first sc, sc in next sc and in ea sc across to last sc, 2 sc in last sc.

Rows 3 and 4: Ch 1, turn; sc in ea sc across.

Rows 5–38 {5–38, 5–44, 5–50}: Rep Rows 2–4, 11 {11, 13, 15} times; then rep Row 2 once more.

Rep Row 3 until Sleeve measures approximately 10¼" {11¼", 12½", 14"} from beg edge; fasten off after last row.

NECK RIBBING

With smaller hook and MC, ch 7 {9, 11, 11} loosely.

Row 1: Sc in 2nd ch from hook and in ea ch across.

Row 2: Ch 1, turn; sc in bk lp only of ea sc across.

Rep Row 2 until ribbing measures approximately 12" {13", 14", 16"} slightly stretched; fasten off after last row.

FINISHING

Cross st plaid design across body sts of Front and Back following *Chart*.

ASSEMBLY

Sew shoulder seams. Sew Sleeves to body matching center of Sleeve to shoulder seam. Sew sleeve and side seams.

Neck Trim: With rs facing and larger hook, join MC with sl st in any st; ch 1, sc in evenly around neck opening; join with sl st to beg sc; fasten off. Sew Neck Ribbing to neck opening.

Chart Key

■ Yellow, A

■ Green, C

■ Lilac, B

Each Square on the charts represents one single crochet stitch.

Chart

X-Lg Lg Med Sm

Chart continued on next page.

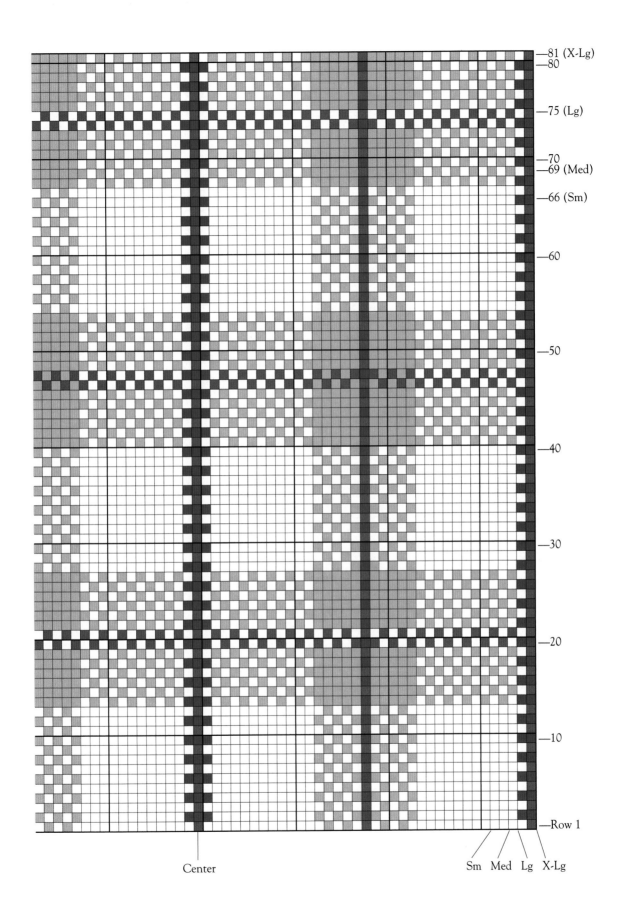

—81 (X-Lg)
—80

—75 (Lg)

—70
—69 (Med)

—66 (Sm)

—60

—50

—40

—30

—20

—10

—Row 1

Center

Sm Med Lg X-Lg

Jewel of a Poncho

This short-cropped poncho is just right for cool autumn days. And its simple styling makes it an easy fashion item to stitch. You're sure to want to make several in a variety of colors!

MATERIALS
Chunky-weight yarn, approximately:
7.5 oz. (345 yd.) variegated
Size N crochet hook or size to obtain gauge

Sizes: Sm/Med and Lg/X-Lg

Size Note: *Instructions are written for size Sm/Med, with Lg/X-Lg in braces { }. Instructions will be easier to read if you highlight all the numbers pertaining to your size. If only one number is given, it applies to all sizes.*

GAUGE
4 Hdc and 3 rows = 2"

Note: *To consolidate the length of this pattern, zeros are sometimes used so that both sizes can be combined. A zero indicates to do nothing until the next group of instructions.*

Ch 46 {51} loosely; being careful not to twist ch, join with sl st to form a ring.

Rnd 1 (rs): Ch 1, hdc in next ch and in ea ch around; do not join, place marker: 45 {50} hdc.

Note: *Move marker at end of ea rnd to mark beg of rnd.*

Rnd 2: * Hdc in next 4 hdc, 2 hdc in next hdc; rep from * around; do not join.

Rnd 3: Hdc in ea hdc around; do not join.

Rnd 4: * Hdc in next 5 hdc, 2 hdc in next hdc; rep from * around; do not join.

Rnd 5: Rep Rnd 3.

Rnd 6: * Hdc in next 6 hdc, 2 hdc in next hdc; rep from * around; do not join.

Rnd 7: Rep Rnd 3.

Rnd 8: * Hdc in next 7 hdc, 2 hdc in next hdc; rep from * around; do not join.

Rnd 9: Rep Rnd 3.

Rnd 10: * Hdc in next 8 hdc, 2 hdc in next hdc; rep from * around; do not join.

Rnd 11: Rep Rnd 3.

Rnd 12: 2 Hdc in next hdc 0 {1} time, hdc in next 49 hdc, 2 hdc in next hdc 0 {1} times, hdc in next hdc and in ea hdc around; do not join.

Rnds 13–25 {13–29}: Hdc in ea hdc around; do not join.

Rnd 26 {30}: * Sc in next hdc, skip next 2 hdc, 5 dc in next hdc, skip next 2 hdc; rep from * around; join with sl st to beg sc; fasten off.

Practice basic crochet stitches by stitching fun and festive ponchos for all of your fashionable friends.

Project was stitched with Jiffy: Denver #307.

Chill-Chasing Pea Coats

The softness and sheen of chenille is shown off to its fullest in these fabulous pea coats.
My son, Nikko, loves his almost as much as I love mine!

MATERIALS
Chunky-weight yarn, approximately:
Child–{400; 500; 600} yd. brown
Adult–[900; 1,000; 1,100] yd. tan
Size P crochet hook or size to obtain gauge
8 (⅞") buttons for child coat
10 (1") buttons for adult coat
Yarn needle

Child's Sizes: Sm, Med, Lg
Finished Measurements: 32", 36", 40"

Adult Sizes: Sm, Med, Lg
Finished Measurements: 42", 46", 50"

Size Note: Instructions are written for Child sizes Sm, Med, and Lg in the first set of braces { } and the Adult sizes Sm, Med, and Lg in brackets [ ]. Instructions will be easier to read if you highlight all the numbers pertaining to your size. If only one number is given, it applies to all sizes.

GAUGE
In pat, 6 hdc and 6 rows = 4"

BACK
Ch {25, 28, 31} [33, 36, 39] loosely.

Row 1 (rs): Hdc in 2nd ch from hook and in ea ch across: {24, 27, 30} [32, 35, 38] hdc.
Note: Mark last row as rs.
Row 2: Ch 1, turn; hdc in ea hdc across.
Rep Row 2 until Back measures approximately {19", 20", 21"} [26", 27", 28"] from beg ch; fasten off after last row.

LEFT FRONT
Ch {17, 20, 23} [23, 26, 29] loosely.

Row 1 (rs): Hdc in 2nd ch from hook and in ea ch across: {16, 19, 22} [22, 25, 28] hdc.
Note: Mark last row as rs.
Rows {2–10} [2–14]: Ch 1, turn; hdc in ea hdc across.
Row {11} [15] (buttonhole row): Ch 1, turn; hdc in first hdc, ch 1, skip next hdc, hdc in next 4 hdc, ch 1, skip next hdc,

> *An attractive comfortable coat is a must for the winter season.*

hdc in last {9, 12, 15} [15, 18, 21] hdc.
Row {12} [16]: Ch 1, turn; hdc in ea hdc and in ea ch-1 sp across.
Rows {13–14} [17–18]: Ch 1, turn; hdc in ea hdc across.
Rows {15–24} [19–32]: Rep Rows {11–14} [15–18], {2} [3] times; then rep Rows {11–12} [15–16] once more.
Row {25} [33]: Turn; sl st in first {5} [7] hdc, ch 1, hdc in next hdc and in ea hdc across: {11, 14, 17} [15, 18, 21] hdc.
Row {26} [34]: Ch 1, turn; hdc in ea hdc across to last hdc, leave last hdc unworked: {10, 13, 16} [14, 17, 20] hdc.
Row {27} [35]: Ch 1, turn; skip first hdc, hdc in next hdc and in ea hdc across: {9, 12, 15} [13, 16, 19] hdc.

For Child Sizes Med and Lg Only
Rows 28–30, 28–32: Rep Rows 26 and 27, {1, 2} time(s): {10, 11} hdc.
For All Child Sizes Only
Row 28, 31, 33: Ch 1, turn; hdc in ea hdc across.
Rep Row 28, 31, 33 until Left Front measures approximately {19", 20", 21"} from beg ch; fasten off after last row.
For Adult Sizes Only
Rows 36–37, 36–39, 36–41: Rep Rows 34 and 35, [1, 2, 3] ➜

time(s): [11, 12, 13] hdc.

Row 38, 40, 42: Ch 1, turn; hdc in ea hdc across.

Rep Row 38, 40, 42 until Left Front measures approximately {26", 27", 28"} from beg ch; fasten off after last row.

RIGHT FRONT

Ch {17, 20, 23} [23, 26, 29] loosely.

Row 1 (rs): Hdc in 2nd ch from hook and in ea ch across: {16, 19, 22} [22, 25, 28] hdc.

Note: Mark last row as rs.

Rows {2–24} [2–32]: Ch 1, turn; hdc in ea hdc across.

Row {25} [33]: Ch 1, turn; hdc in ea hdc across to last {5} [7] hdc, leave last {5} [7] hdc unworked: {11, 14, 17} [15, 18, 21].

Row {26} [34]: Ch 1, turn; skip first hdc, hdc in next hdc and in ea hdc across: {10, 13, 16} [14, 17, 20] hdc.

Row {27} [35]: Ch 1, turn; hdc in ea hdc across to last hdc, leave last hdc unworked: {9, 12, 15} [13, 16, 19] hdc.

For Child Sizes Med and Lg Only

Rows 28–30, 28–32: Rep Rows 26 and 27, {1, 2} time(s): {10, 11} hdc.

For All Child Sizes Only

Row 28, 31, 33: Ch 1, turn; hdc in ea hdc across.

Rep Row 28, 31, 33 until Left Front measures approximately {19", 20", 21"} from beg ch; fasten off after last row.

For Adult Sizes Only

Rows 36–37, 36–39, 36–41: Rep Rows 34 and 35, [1, 2, 3]

time(s): [11, 12, 13] hdc.

Row 38, 40, 42: Ch 1, turn; hdc in ea hdc across.

Rep Row 38, 40, 42 until Right Front measures approximately [26", 27", 28"] from beg ch; fasten off after last row.

SLEEVE (MAKE 2.)

Ch {18, 21, 24} [24, 27, 30] loosely.

Row 1 (rs): Hdc in 2nd ch from hook and in ea ch across: {17, 20, 23} [23, 26, 29] hdc.

Note: Mark last row as rs.

Rows {2–7} [2–12, 2–13, 2–14]: Ch 1, turn; hdc in ea hdc across.

Row {8} [13, 14, 15]: Ch 1, turn; 2 hdc in first hdc, hdc in next hdc and in ea hdc across to last hdc, 2 hdc in last hdc: {19, 22, 25} [25, 28, 31] hdc.

Rows {9–14} [14–17; 15–18; 16–19]: Ch 1, turn; hdc in ea hdc across.

Row {15} [18, 19, 20]: Rep Row {8} [13, 14, 15]: {21, 24, 27} [27, 30, 33] hdc.

Row {16} [19, 20, 21]: Ch 1, turn; hdc in ea hdc across.

Rep Row {16} [19, 20, 21] until Sleeve measures approximately {14", 15", 16"} [17", 18", 19"] from beg ch; fasten off after last row.

COLLAR

Ch {29, 32, 35} [44, 47, 50] loosely.

Row 1: Hdc in 2nd ch from hook and in ea ch across.

Rows {2–6, 2–7, 2–7} [2–9, 2–10, 2–10]: Ch 1, turn; hdc in ea hdc across; fasten off after last row.

POCKET (MAKE 2.)

Ch {9} [10] loosely.

Row 1: Hdc in 2nd ch from hook and in ea ch across: {8} [9] hdc.

Rows {2–5} [2–9]: Ch 1, turn; hdc in ea hdc across.

Row {6} [10]: Ch 1, turn; hdc in ea hdc across to last hdc, leave last hdc unworked: {7} [8] hdc.

Row {7} [11]: Ch 1, turn; skip first hdc, hdc in next hdc and in ea hdc across: {6} [7] hdc.

Rows {8–11} [12–15]: Rep Rows {6–7} [10–11], twice; fasten off after last row.

FINISHING

Sew shoulder seams. Sew Sleeves to body matching center of Sleeve to shoulder seam. Sew sleeve and side seams. Sew Collar to neckline easing into place. Sew Pockets to fronts. Sew buttons to Right Front matching buttonholes.

TRIM

Jacket: With rs facing, join yarn with sl st in any st; ch 1, sc evenly around entire jacket; join with sl st to beg sc; fasten off.

Sleeve: Join yarn with sl st in free lp of any ch; ch 1, sc in same st as joining and in ea st around; join with sl st to beg sc; fasten off.

Rep for 2nd Sleeve.

Projects were stitched with Chenille Thick & Quick: Chocolate #125, Champagne #155.

Summer Sunset Wrap

A well-designed wrap like this can add an air of sophistication to any ensemble. And the design lends itself equally well to bold, playful hues or to conservative, understated shades.

MATERIALS

Sportweight yarn, approximately:
15 oz. (1,010 yd.) orange
Size I crochet hook or size to obtain gauge

FINISHED SIZE

Approximately 25" x 36"

GAUGE

In pat, 4 dc = 1"
Point to point = 3¼"

Ch 92 loosely.

Row 1: Dc in 4th ch from hook and in next 4 chs, * skip next 2 chs, dc in next 4 chs **, 3 dc in next ch, dc in next 4 chs; rep from * across, ending last rep at **, 2 dc in last ch.

Row 2: Ch 3 [counts as first dc], turn; dc in first 5 dc, * skip next 2 dc, dc in next 4 dc **, 3 dc in next dc, dc in next 4 dc; rep from * across, ending last rep at **, 2 dc in next ch.

Rep Row 2 until wrap measures approximately 60" from beg ch; fasten off after last row.

Project was stitched with Microspun: Mango #186.

Elegant Evenings Tunic

The picot edging gives a finishing touch to this lovely openwork tunic. Wear a form-fitting shell underneath in a matching color for a very tailored look—or pick a contrasting color to really highlight the beautiful crochet stitches.

MATERIALS

Sportweight yarn, approximately:
20 {20, 25, 25} oz. (1,740 {1,740; 2,175; 2,175} yd.) white
Size H crochet hook or size to obtain gauge
Yarn needle

Sizes: Sm, Med, Lg, X-Lg
Finished Measurements: 36", 40", 45", 49"

Size Note: *Instructions are written for size Sm, with sizes Med, Lg, and X-Lg in braces { }. Instructions will be easier to read if you highlight all the numbers pertaining to your size. If only one number is given, it applies to all sizes.*

GAUGE

In pat, 4 rep = 4½"; 6 rows = 3"

PATTERN STITCH

Picot: Ch 3, sl st in top of last sc made.

BACK

Ch 84 {94, 104, 114}.
Row 1 (rs): (4 Dc, ch 3, dc) in 6th ch from hook, * skip next 4 chs, (4 dc, ch 3, dc) in next ch; rep from * across to last 3 chs, skip next 2 chs, dc in last ch.
Note: *Mark last row as rs.*
Row 2: Ch 3 [counts as first dc], turn; (4 dc, ch 3, dc) in ea ch-3 sp across, skip next 4 dc, dc in next ch.
Rep Row 2 until Back measures approximately 14" from beg ch.

Armhole Shaping

Row 1: Ch 1, turn; sl st in first 14 sts, ch 3, (4 dc, ch 3, dc) in ea ch-3 sp across to last 2 ch-3 sps, skip next 4 dc, dc in next dc, leave rem sts unworked.
Row 2: Ch 3, turn; (4 dc, ch 3, dc) in ea ch-3 sp across, skip next 4 dc, dc in next ch.
Rep Row 2 until Back measures approximately 22" {22", 23", 23"} from beg ch, ending by working a ws row.

Neck Shaping

Right Side
Row 1: Ch 1, turn; sl st in first 9 sts, ch 3, (4 dc, ch 3, dc) in ea of next 2 {3, 3, 4} ch-3 sps, 3 dc in next ch-3 sp, skip next 4 dc, dc in next dc, leave rem sts unworked.
Row 2: Ch 3, turn; (4 dc, ch 3, dc) in ea of next 1 {2, 2, 3} ch-3 sp(s), 4 hdc in next ch-3 sp, skip next 3 dc, sl st in next dc; fasten off.

Left Side
Row 1: With ws facing, skip next 4 {4, 6, 6} ch-3 sps from Right Side edge, join yarn with sl st in next dc; ch 3, (dc, ch 3, dc) in next ch-3 sp, (4 dc, ch 3, dc) in ea of next 2 {3, 3, 4} ch-3 sps, skip next 4 dc, dc in next dc, leave rem sts unworked.
Row 2: Ch 1, turn; skip first dc, sl st in next dc, 3 hdc in next ch-3 sp, (4 dc, ch 3, dc) in ea of next 1 {2, 2, 3} ch-3 sps, 2 dc in last ch-3 sp; fasten off.

FRONT

Work as for Back until Front measures approximately 19" {19", 20", 20"} from beg ch, ending by working a rs row.
Neck Shaping
Right Side
Row 1: Ch 3, turn; (4 dc, ch 3, dc) in ea of next 3 {4, 5, 6} ch-3 sps, skip next 4 dc, dc in next ➜

Project was stitched with Wool-Ease Sportweight White/Multi: #301 dc, leave rem sts unworked.

Rows 2–3 {2–3, 2–5, 2–5}: Ch 3, turn; (4 dc, ch 3, dc) in ea ch-3 sp across, skip next 4 dc, dc in next ch.

Row 4 {4, 6, 6}: Ch 3, turn; (dc, ch 3, dc) in next ch-3 sp, (4 dc, ch 3, dc) in ea of next 2 {3, 3, 4} ch-3 sps, skip next 4 dc, dc in next dc, leave rem sts unworked.

Row 5 {5, 7, 7}: Ch 1, turn; skip first dc, sl st in next dc, 3 hdc in next ch-3 sp, (4 dc, ch 3, dc) in ea of next 1 {2, 2, 3} ch-3 sp(s), 2 dc in last ch-3 sp; fasten off.

Left side

Row 1: With ws facing, skip next 4 {4, 6, 6} ch-3 sps from Right Side edge, join yarn with sl st in next dc; ch 3, (4 dc, ch 3, dc) in next 3 {4, 5, 6} ch-3 sps, skip next 4 dc, dc in next ch.

Rows 2–3 {2–3, 2–5, 2–5}: Ch 3, turn; (4 dc, ch 3, dc) in ea ch-3 sp across, skip next 4 dc, dc in next ch.

Row 4 {4, 6, 6}: Ch 1, turn; sl st in first 9 sts, ch 3, (4 dc, ch 3, dc) in ea of next 2 {3, 3, 4} ch-3 sps, 3 dc in next ch-3 sp, skip next 4 dc, dc in next ch.

Row 5 {5, 7, 7}: Ch 3, turn; (4 dc, ch 3, dc) in ea of next 1 {2, 2, 3} ch-3 sps, 4 hdc in next ch-3 sp, skip next 3 dc, sl st in next dc; fasten off.

SLEEVE (MAKE 2.)
Ch 44 {44, 54, 54}.

Row 1 (rs): (4 Dc, ch 3, dc) in 6th ch from hook, * skip next 4 chs, (4 dc, ch 3, dc) in next ch; rep from * across to last 3 chs, skip next 2 chs, dc in last ch.

Row 2: Ch 3, turn; (4 dc, ch 3, dc) in ea ch-3 sp across, skip next 4 dc, dc in next ch.

Row 3: Ch 3, turn; dc in first dc, (4 dc, ch 3, dc) in ea ch-3 sp across, skip next 4 dc, 2 dc in next ch.

Row 4: Ch 3, turn; skip first dc, 2 dc in next dc, (4 dc, ch 3, dc) in ea ch-3 sp across, skip next 4 dc, 2 dc in next dc, dc in next ch.

Row 5: Ch 3, turn; dc in first 3 dc, (4 dc, ch 3, dc) in ea ch-3 sp across, skip next 4 dc, dc in next 2 dc, 2 dc in next ch.

Row 6: Ch 3, turn; skip first dc, dc in next dc, skip next dc, (dc, ch 3, dc) in next dc, (4 dc, ch 3, dc) in ea ch-3 sp across, skip next 4 dc, (dc, ch 3, dc) in next dc, skip next dc, dc in next 2 sts.

Row 7: Ch 3, turn; (4 dc, ch 3, dc) in ea ch-3 sp across, skip next 2 dc, dc in next ch.

Row 8: Ch 3, turn; (4 dc, ch 3, dc) in ea ch-3 sp across, skip next 4 dc, dc in next ch.

Rows 9–13: Rep Rows 3–7.

Rep Row 8 until Sleeve measures approximately 17½" {18", 18¼", 18½"} from beg ch; fasten off after last row.

FINISHING
Sew shoulder seams. Sew Sleeves to body matching center of Sleeve to shoulder seam. Sew sleeve and side seams.

TRIM
Body: With rs facing and working across bottom edge, join yarn with sl st in any sp; ch 1, (2 sc, picot, 2 sc) in same sp as joining, sc in free lp of next ch, picot, * (2 sc, picot, 2 sc) in next sp, sc in free lp of next ch, picot; rep from * around; join with sl st to beg sc; fasten off.

Neck: With rs facing, join yarn with sl st in first unworked ch-3 sp on Back; work (3 sc, picot) evenly around Neck opening; join with sl st to beg sc; fasten off.

Sleeve: With rs facing and working across bottom edge, join yarn with sl st in any sp; ch 1, (2 sc, picot, 2 sc) in same sp as joining, sc in free lp of next ch, picot, * (2 sc, picot, 2 sc) in next sp, sc in free lp of next ch, picot; rep from * around; join with sl st to beg sc; fasten off.

Rep for 2nd Sleeve.

Mother-Daughter Duet

It's not always easy to find matching outfits that look equally wonderful on both mother and daughter. That's why I was so delighted with this set. Giovanna looks precious in her dress, and while my tunic coordinates with her, I don't have to look like a little girl myself!

TUNIC

MATERIALS

Sportweight yarn,
    approximately:
12½ {15, 17½, 20} oz. (840
    {1,010; 1,175; 1,345} yd.)
    coral
Size H crochet hook or size
    to obtain gauge
Yarn needle

Sizes: Sm, Med, Lg, X-Lg
Finished Measurements: 36",
40", 44", 48"

Size Note: Instructions are written for size Sm, with sizes Med, Lg, and X-Lg in braces { }. Instructions will be easier to read if you highlight all the numbers pertaining to your size. If only one number is given, it applies to all sizes.

GAUGE

In pat, 9 sc = 2" and 10
rows = 3"

BACK

Ch 78 {84, 96, 102} loosely.
Row 1 (rs): Sc in 2nd ch from
hook and in ea ch across: 77 {83,
95, 101} sc.
Note: *Mark last row as rs.*

Row 2: Ch 3 [counts as first dc throughout], turn; skip first 2 sc, (dc, ch 1, dc) in next sc, * skip next 2 sc, (dc, ch 1, dc) in next sc; rep from * across to last 2 sc, skip next sc, dc in last sc: 52 {56, 64, 68} dc and 25 {27, 31, 33} sps.
Row 3: Ch 1, turn; sc in ea dc and in ea ch-1 sp across: 77 {83, 95, 101} sc.

Rep Rows 2 and 3 until Back measures approximately 20" {21", 22", 23"} from beg ch, ending by working Row 2.

Trim

Row 1 (ws): Ch 1, do not turn; 2 sc in end of last row made, (sc in next row, 2 sc in next row) across to last row, skip last row, 3 sc in ch at base of first sc, sc in ea ch across to last ch, 3 sc in last ch, skip end of first row, 2 sc in next row, (sc in next row, 2 sc in next row) across; do not work across last row.

For Sizes Sm and Lg Only
Row 2 (rs): Ch 1, turn; sc in ea sc across working 3 sc in ea bottom corner; fasten off.

For Sizes Med and X-Lg Only
Rows 2 and 3: Ch 1, turn; sc in ea sc across working 3 sc in ea bottom corner; fasten off after last row.

FRONT
Body
Work same as Back until piece measures approximately 14" {15", 16", 17"} from beg ch, ending by working Row 3.

Right Front
Row 1 (ws): Ch 3, turn; skip first 2 sc, (dc, ch 1, dc) in next sc, * skip next 2 sc, (dc, ch 1, dc) in next sc; rep from * 10 {11, 13, 14} times more, skip next dc, dc in next sc, leave rem sts unworked: 26 {28, 32, 34} dc and 12 {13, 15, 16} sps.
Row 2: Ch 1, turn; sc in ea dc and in ea ch-1 sp across: 38 {41, 47, 50} sc.
Row 3: Ch 3, turn; skip first 2 sc, (dc, ch 1, dc) in next sc, * skip next 2 sc, (dc, ch 1, dc) in next sc; rep from * across to last 2 sc, skip next sc, dc in last sc: 26 {28, 32, 34} dc and 12 {13, 15, 16} sps.
Rows 4–8: Rep Rows 2 and 3 twice; then rep Row 2 once more.
Row 9: Ch 3, turn; skip first 2 sc, (dc, ch 1, dc) in next sc, * skip next 2 sc, (dc, ch 1, dc) in next sc; rep from * 5 {6, 7, 8} times more, skip next sc, dc in next sc, leave rem sts unworked: 16 {18, 20, 22} dc ➔

and 7 {8, 9, 10} sps.

Row 10: Ch 1, turn; sc in ea dc and in ea ch-1 sp across: 23 {26, 29, 32} sc.

Row 11: Ch 3, turn; skip first 2 sc, (dc, ch 1, dc) in next sc, * skip next 2 sc, (dc, ch 1, dc) in next sc; rep from * across to last 2 sc, skip next sc, dc in last sc: 16 {18, 20, 22} dc and 7 {8, 9, 10} sps.

Rows 12–14 {12–16, 12–18, 12–20}: Rep Rows 10 and 11, 1 {2, 3, 4} time(s); then rep Row 10 once more; fasten off at end of last row.

Left Front

Row 1: With ws facing, skip next sc from last dc worked on Row 1 of Right Front edge, join yarn with sl st in next sc; ch 3, skip next dc, (dc, ch 1, dc) in next sc, * skip next 2 sc, (dc, ch 1 dc) in next sc; rep from * across to last 2 sc, skip next sc, dc in last sc: 26 {28, 32, 34} dc and 12 {13, 15, 16} sps.

Rows 2–8: Work same as Right Front.

Row 9: Turn; sl st in first 16 {16, 19, 19} sc, ch 3, skip next sc, (dc, ch 1, dc) in next sc, * skip next 2 sc, (dc, ch 1, dc) in next sc; rep from * across to last 2 sc, skip next sc, dc in next sc: 16 {18, 20, 22} dc and 7 {8, 9, 10} sps.

Rows 10–14 {10–16, 10–18, 10–20}: Work same as Right Front.

SLEEVE (MAKE 2.)
Ch 54 {57, 60, 63} loosely.

Row 1 (rs): Sc in 2nd ch from hook and in ea ch across: 53 {56, 59, 62} sc.

Note: Mark last row as rs.

Row 2: Ch 3, turn; skip first 2 sc, (dc, ch 1, dc) in next sc, * skip next 2 sc, (dc, ch 1, dc) in next sc; rep from * across to last 2 sc, skip next sc, dc in last sc: 36 {38, 40, 42} dc and 17 {18, 19, 20} sps.

Rows 3–22: Ch 3, turn; (dc, ch 1, dc) in ea ch-1 sp across, skip next dc, dc in last dc.

Rows 23–24: Ch 3, turn; (dc, ch 1, 2 dc, ch 1, dc) in first ch-1 sp, (dc, ch 1, dc) in ea ch-1 sp across, skip next dc, dc in last dc: 40 {42, 44, 46} dc and 19 {20, 21, 22} sps.

Rows 25–34: Rep Row 3.

Row 35: Ch 3, turn; (dc, ch 1, 2 dc, ch 1, dc) in first ch-1 sp, (dc, ch 1, dc) in ea ch-1 sp across to last ch-1 sp, (dc, ch 1, 2 dc, ch 1, dc) in last ch-1 sp, skip next dc, dc in last dc: 44 {46, 48, 50} dc and 21 {22, 23, 24} sps.

Row 36: Rep Row 3.

Row 37: Rep Row 35.

Rows 38–39: Rep Row 3; fasten off after last row.

FINISHING
Sew shoulder seams.
Sew sleeves to tunic.
Sew sleeve and side seams, leaving 2½" opening at bottom edge open for side slit.

TRIM
Neck Edging: With rs of back facing, join yarn with sl st in any st; ch 1, sc evenly around neck edge and front placket opening; join with sl st to beg sc; fasten off.

SLEEVE EDGING
Rnd 1: With rs facing, join yarn with sl st in seam; ch 1, sc in same sp as joining 1 {2, 1, 1} time(s), sc in free lp of ea ch around; join with sl st to beg sc: 54 {58, 60, 62} sc.

Rnd 2: * (Sl st, ch 3, sl st) in next sc, sl st in next sc; rep from * around; fasten off.

Rep for 2nd sleeve.

Projects were stitched with Microspun: Coral #103.

DRESS

MATERIALS

Sportweight yarn,
approximately:
12½ {15, 17½} oz. (840
{1,010; 1,175} yd.) coral
Size H crochet hook or size
to obtain gauge
⅛" ribbon 60" length

Sizes: Sm, Med, Lg
Finished Chest Measurements:
22", 24", 26"

*Size Note: Instructions are written
for size Sm, with sizes Med and Lg
in braces { }. Instructions will be
easier to read if you highlight all the
numbers pertaining to your size. If
only one number is given, it applies
to all sizes.*

GAUGE
In pat, 8 sc and 6 rnds = 2"

*Note: To consolidate the length of
this pattern. Zeros are sometimes
used so that all sizes can be combined. A zero indicated to do
nothing until the next group of
instructions.*

BODY
Ch 147 {156, 165} loosely, being
careful not to twist ch; join with
sl st to form a ring.
Rnd 1 (rs): Ch 1, sc in same st
as joining and in ea ch around;
join with sl st to beg sc: 147

{156, 165} sc.
Note: Mark last rnd as rs.
Rnd 2: Ch 4, dc in same st as
joining, skip next 2 sc, * (dc,
ch 1, dc) in next sc, skip next
2 sc; rep from * around; join
with sl st to 3rd ch of beg ch-4.
Rnd 3: Ch 1, turn; sc in same st
as joining and in ea dc and ea
ch-1 sp around; join with sl st
to beg sc.
Rnd 4: Ch 1, turn; skip first sc,
sl st, ch 4, dc in next sc, skip
next 2 sc, * (dc, ch 1, dc) in
next sc, skip next 2 sc; rep from
* around; join with sl st to 3rd
ch of beg ch-4.
Rep Rnds 3 and 4 until skirt
measures approximately 17" {18",
19"} from beg ch, ending by
working row 3.
Next Rnd: Ch 1, turn; sc in
ea sc around; join with sl st to
beg sc.
Dec Rnd (eyelet rnd): Ch 3,
turn; skip first 2 sc, dc in next sc,
skip next sc, dc in next sc, skip
next 2 sc, dc in next sc, * (skip

next sc, dc in next sc) twice,
skip next 2 sc, dc in next sc; rep
from * around to last 6 {1, 3} sc,
skip next 1 {0, 1} sc, dc in next
sc, skip next 1 {0, 0} sc, dc in
next 1 {0, 1} sc, skip next 1 {0, 0}
sc, dc in next 1 {0, 0} sc; join
with sl st to 3rd ch of beg ch-3:
64 {68, 72} sts.

BODICE
Rnd 1: Ch 1, turn; sc in ea dc
around; join with sl st to beg sc.
Rnd 2: Ch 1, turn; sc in next 8
{9, 10} sc, ch 28 [armhole], skip
next 16 sc, sc in next 16 {18, 20}
sc, ch 28 [armhole], skip next
16 sc, sc in last 8 {9, 10} sc; join
with sl st to beg sc.
Rnd 3: Ch 1, turn; sc in ea sc
and in ea ch around; join with sl
st to beg sc: 88 {92, 96} sc.
Rnd 4: Ch 1, turn; sc in next
8 {9, 10} sc, * skip next sc, sc in
next 26 sc, skip next sc **, sc in
next 16 {18, 20} sc; rep from * to
** once, sc in last 8 {9, 10} sc;
join with sl st to beg sc. ➜

Rnd 5: Ch 1, turn; sc in next 8 {9, 10} sc, * skip next sc, sc in next 24 sc, skip next sc **, sc in next 16 {18, 20} sc; rep from * to ** once, sc in last 8 {9, 10} sc; join with sl st to beg sc.

Rnd 6: Ch 1, turn; sc in next 8 {9, 10} sc, * skip next sc, sc in next 22 sc, skip next sc **, sc in next 16 {18, 20} sc; rep from * to ** once, sc in last 8 {9, 10} sc; join with sl st to beg sc.

Rnd 7: Ch 1, turn; sc in next 8 {9, 10} sc, * skip next sc, sc in next 20 sc, skip next sc **, sc in next 16 {18, 20} sc; rep from * to ** once, sc in last 8 {9, 10} sc; join with sl st to beg sc.

Rnd 8: Ch 1, turn; sc in next 8 {9, 10} sc, * skip next sc, sc in next 18 sc, skip next sc **, sc in next 16 {18, 20} sc; rep from * to ** once, sc in last 8 {9, 10} sc; join with sl st to beg sc.

Rnd 9: Ch 1, turn; sc in next 8 {9, 10} sc, * skip next sc, sc in next 16 sc, skip next sc **, sc in next 16 {18, 20} sc; rep from * to ** once, sc in last 8 {9, 10} sc; join with sl st to beg sc.

Rnd 10: Ch 1, turn; sc in next sc and in ea sc around; join with sl st to beg sc.

Rnd 11: Ch 1, do not turn; * (sl st, ch 3, sl st) in next sc, sl st in next sc; rep from * around; join with sl st to beg sl st; fasten off.

SLEEVE

Rnd 1 (rs): With rs facing, join yarn with sl st in first skipped sc at armhole; ch 4, dc in same st as joining, [skip next 2 sc, (dc, ch 1, dc) in next sc] 5 times, skip end of next row, (dc, ch 1, dc) in free lp of next ch, skip next 2 chs, (dc, ch 1, dc) in free lp of next ch] 9 times; join with sl st to 3rd ch of beg ch-4.

Rnds 2–5: (Sl st, ch 4, dc) in next ch-1 sp, (dc, ch 1, dc) in ea ch-1 sp around; join with sl st to 3rd ch of beg ch-4.

Rnd 6: Ch 1, sc in same st as joining and in ea ch-1 sp and ea dc around; join with sl st to beg sc.

Rnd 7: * (Sl st, ch 3, sl st) in next sc, sl st in next sc; rep from * around; join with sl st to beg sl st; fasten off.

Rep for second sleeve.

FINISHING
Skirt Edging
Rnd 1 (rs): With rs facing, join yarn with sl st in free lp of any ch; ch 1, sc in same ch as joining and in ea ch around; join with sl st to beg sc: 147 {156, 165} sc.

Rnd 2: Ch 4, dc in same st as joining, skip next 2 sc, * (dc, ch 1, dc) in next sc, skip next 2 sc; rep from * around; join with sl st to 3rd ch of beg ch-4.

Rnd 3: (Sl st, ch 4, dc) in next ch-1 sp, (dc, ch 1, dc) in ea ch-1 sp around; join with sl st to 3rd ch of beg ch-4.

Rnd 4: Ch 1, 2 {1, 2} sc in same st as joining, sc in ea sc around; join with sl st to beg sc.

Rnd 5: * (Sl st, ch 3, sl st) in next sc, sl st in next sc; rep from * around; join with sl st to beg sl st; fasten off.

Weave ribbon through eyelet rnd and tie in a bow at center front.

Be sure to use a soft, lightweight yarn to make the dress so that it will be a cool and comfortable outfit for hot summer days.

General Directions

Crochet Abbreviations

beg	begin(ning)	ft lp(s)	front loop(s)	st(s)	stitch(es)
bet	between	grp(s)	group(s)	tch	turning chain
bk lp(s)	back loop(s)	hdc	half double crochet	tog	together
ch	chain(s)	inc	increas(es) (ed) (ing)	tr	triple crochet
ch-	refers to chain previously made	lp(s)	loop(s)	yo	yarn over
cl	cluster(s)	pat(s)	pattern(s)		
cont	continu(e) (ing)	prev	previous		
dc	double crochet	rem	remain(s) (ing)		
dec	decreas(es) (ed) (ing)	rep	repeat(s)		
dtr	double triple crochet	rnd(s)	round(s)		
ea	each	sc	single crochet		
est	established	sk	skip(ped)		
foll	follow(s) (ing)	sl st	slip stitch		
		sp(s)	space(s)		

Repeat whatever follows * as indicated. "Rep from * 3 times more" means to work 4 times in all.

Work directions given in parentheses ( ) and brackets [ ] the number of times specified or in the place specified.

Aluminum Crochet Hook Sizes

U.S.	Size	Metric	Canada/U.K.	U.S.	Size	Metric	Canada/U.K.
B	(1)	2.25	13	H	(8)	5.00	6
C	(2)	2.75		I	(9)	5.50	5
D	(3)	3.25	10	J	(10)	6.00	4
E	(4)	3.50	9	K	(10½)	6.50	3
F	(5)	4.00		N		10.00	000
G	(6)	4.25	8				

Metric Conversion
Common Measures

⅛" = 3 mm	5" = 12.7 cm	⅛ yard = 0.11 m
¼" = 6 mm	6" = 15.2 cm	¼ yard = 0.23 m
⅜" = 9 mm	7" = 17.8 cm	⅓ yard = 0.3 m
½" = 1.3 cm	8" = 20.3 cm	⅜ yard = 0.34 m
⅝" = 1.6 cm	9" = 22.9 cm	½ yard = 0.46 m
¾" = 1.9 cm	10" = 25.4 cm	⅝ yard = 0.57 m
⅞" = 2.2 cm	11" = 27.9 cm	⅔ yard = 0.61 m
1" = 2.5 cm	12" = 30.5 cm	¾ yard = 0.69 m
2" = 5.1 cm	36" = 91.5 cm	⅞ yard = 0.8 m
3" = 7.6 cm	45" = 114.3 cm	1 yard = 0.91 m
4" = 10.2 cm	60" = 152.4 cm	

A Note to Left-Handed Crocheters

Since instructions for crocheted projects most often appear with right-handed instructions only, it may be worth your while to learn right-handed crochet techniques. Since the work is shared between the hands in crochet, it may be surprisingly easy for you to make use of the accompanying diagrams. If working in this way is not comfortable, use a mirror to reverse the diagrams or reverse them on a photocopier.

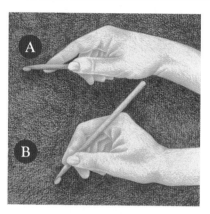

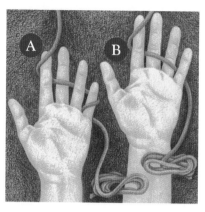

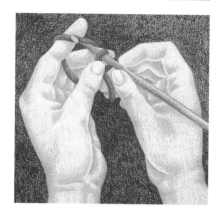

Holding the Hook

Hold the hook as you would a piece of chalk (**A**) or a pencil (**B**). If your hook has a finger rest, position your thumb and opposing finger there for extra control.

Holding the Yarn

Weave the yarn through the fingers of your left hand. Some people like to wrap the yarn around the little finger for extra control (**A**); some do not (**B**). In either case, the forefinger plays the most important role in regulating tension as yarn is fed into the work.

Working Together

Once work has begun, the thumb and the middle finger of the left hand come into play, pressing together to hold the stitches just made.

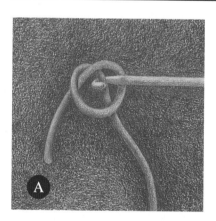

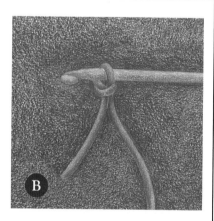

Slip Knot

A. Loop the yarn around and let the loose end of the yarn fall behind the loop to form a pretzel shape as shown. Insert the hook.

B. Pull both ends to close the knot.

Gauge

Before beginning a project, work a 4"-square gauge swatch, using the recommended size hook. Count and compare the number of stitches per inch in the swatch with the designer's gauge. If you have fewer stitches in your swatch, try a smaller hook; if you have more stitches, try a larger hook.

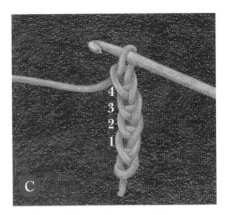

Chain Stitch

A. Place slip knot on hook. With thumb and middle finger of left hand holding yarn end, wrap yarn up and over hook (from back to front). This movement is called "yarn over" (yo) and is basic to every crochet stitch.

B. Use hook to pull yarn through loop (lp) already on hook. Combination of yo and pulling yarn through lp makes 1 chain stitch (ch).

C. Repeat A and B until ch is desired length. Try to keep movements even and relaxed and all ch stitches (sts) same size. Hold ch near working area to keep it from twisting. Count sts as shown in diagram. (Do not count lp on hook or slip knot.)

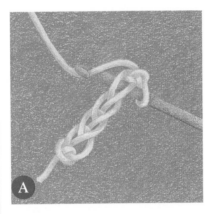

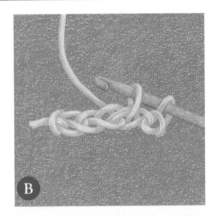

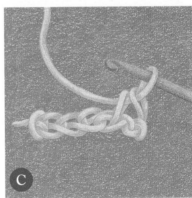

Slip Stitch

Here slip stitch (sl st) is used to join ring. Taking care not to twist chain, insert hook into first ch made, yo and pull through ch and lp on hook (sl st made). Sl st can also be used to join finished pieces or to move across groups of sts without adding height to work.

Single Crochet

A. Insert hook under top 2 lps of 2nd ch from hook and yo. (Always work sts through top 2 lps unless directions specify otherwise.)
B. Yo and pull yarn through ch (2 lps on hook).
C. Yo and pull yarn through 2 lps on hook (1 sc made).

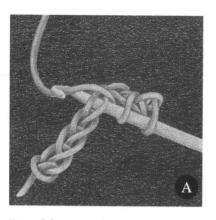

Double Crochet

A. Yo, insert hook into 4th ch from hook, and yo.

B. Yo and pull yarn through ch (3 lps on hook).

C. Yo and pull through 2 lps on hook (2 lps remaining).

D. Yo and pull through 2 remaining (rem) lps (1 dc made).

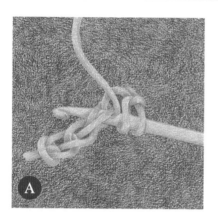

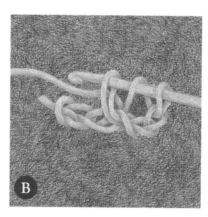

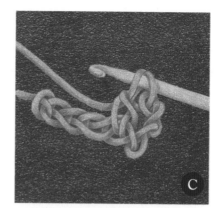

Half-Double Crochet

A. Yo and insert hook into 3rd ch from hook.

B. Yo and pull through ch (3 lps on hook).

C. Yo and pull yarn through all 3 lps on hook (1 hdc made).

Triple Crochet

A. Yo twice, insert hook into 5th ch from hook. Yo and pull through ch (4 lps on hook).
B. Yo and pull through 2 lps on hook (3 lps rem). Yo and pull through 2 lps on hook (2 lps rem). Yo and pull through 2 lps on hook (1 tr made).

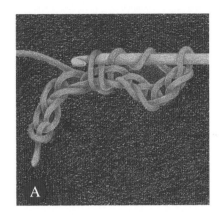

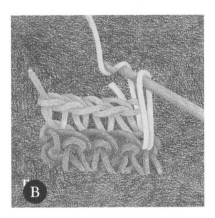

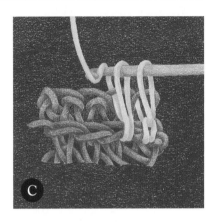

Assembly

To assemble crocheted pieces, use a large-eyed yarn needle to whip-stitch (**A**) or a crochet hook to slip stitch (**B**) the pieces together. Pieces can also be joined using single crochet stitches (**C**), but this makes a heavier seam.

When making squares or other pieces to be stitched together, leave a 20" tail of yarn when fastening off. This yarn tail can then be used to stitch the pieces together, with all stitches and rows of the squares or the strips aligned and running in the same direction.

Joining Yarn

To change colors or to begin a new skein of yarn at the end of a row, work the last yarn over for the last stitch of the previous row with the new yarn.

Fastening Off

Cut the yarn, leaving a 6" tail. Yarn over and pull the tail through the last loop on the hook. Thread the tail into a large-eyed yarn needle and weave it carefully into the back of the work.

Metric Math

When you know:	Multiply by:	To find:	When you know:	Multiply by:	To find:
inches (")	25	millimeters (mm)	millimeters (mm)	0.039	inches (")
inches (")	2.5	centimeters (cm)	centimeters (cm)	0.39	inches (")
inches (")	0.025	meters (m)	meters (m)	39	inches (")
yards (yd.)	0.9	meters (m)	meters (m)	1.093	yards (yd.)
ounces (oz.)	28.35	grams (g)			

Loop Stitch (lp st)

A. With wrong side (ws) of work facing, insert hook in next st. Wrap yarn over ruler or index finger to form 1"-high lp. Pick up bottom strand of yarn with hook and pull through st, keeping lp taut.
B. Yo and pull through both lps on hook to complete st as a sc.

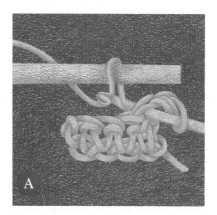 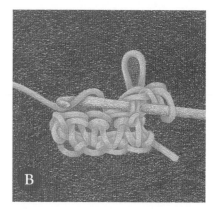

Front Post dc (FPdc)

A. Yo and insert hook from front to back around post of st on previous row.
B. Complete dc st as usual. (Back post dc [BPdc] is worked in same manner, except you insert hook from back to front around post.)

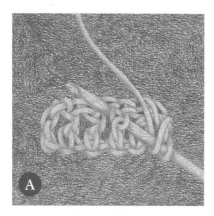 

Basic Popcorn

A. Work 5 dc in st indicated, drop lp from hook, and insert hook in first dc of 5-dc grp.
B. Pick up dropped lp and pull through.

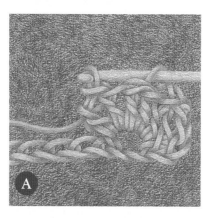 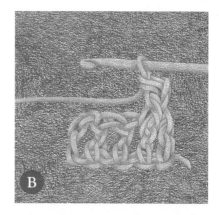

Working in Back Loops Only.

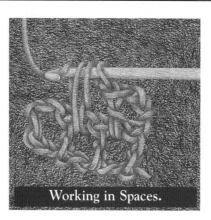
Working in Spaces.

Working Between Stiches.

Stitch Placement Variations

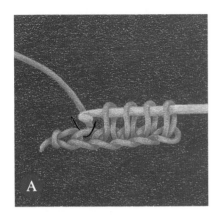

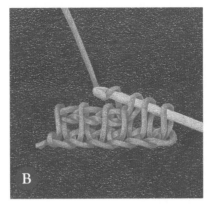

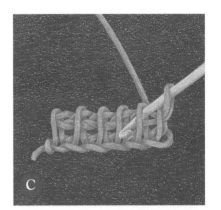

Afghan Stitch

A. *Row 1: Step 1:* Keeping all lps on hook, pull up lp through top lp only in 2nd ch from hook and in ea ch across = same number of lps and chs. Do not turn.

B. *Step 2:* Yo and pull through first lp on hook, * yo and pull through 2 lps on hook, rep from * across (1 lp rem on hook for first lp of next row). Do not turn.

C. *Row 2: Step 1:* Keeping all lps on hook, pull up lp from under 2nd vertical bar, * pull up lp from under next vertical bar, rep from * across. Do not turn. *Step 2:* Rep step 2 of Row 1.

Rep both steps of Row 2 for required number of rows. Fasten off after last row by working sl st in ea bar across.

D. Finished fabric is perfect grid for cross-stitch.

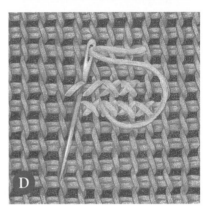

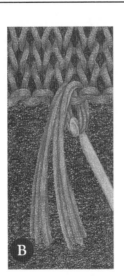

Fringe

To make a simple fringe, cut the required number of yarn lengths as specified in the directions.

Insert the hook through 1 stitch at the edge of the afghan and fold the yarn lengths in half over the hook (**A**). Pull the folded yarn partway through the stitch to form a loop (**B**). Pull the yarn ends through the loop (**C**) and pull tight (**D**).

Acknowledgments

LION BRAND® YARNS

Al•Pa•Ka (Article #740)
Worsted-weight yarn
30% alpaka, 30% wool, 40% acrylic
1¾-oz. (107-yd.) balls

Babysoft (Article #920)
Sport-weight yarn
60% acrylic, 40% polyamid
Solids: 5-oz. (459-yd.) balls
Prints: 4-oz. (367-yd.) balls

Chenille Sensations (Article #730)
Worsted-weight yarn
100% Monsanto acrylic
1.4-oz. (87-yd.) skeins

Chenille Thick & Quick® (Article #950)
Chunky-weight yarn
91% acrylic, 9% rayon
Solids: 100-yd. skeins
Prints: 75-yd. skeins

Homespun® (Article #790)
Chunky-weight yarn
98% acrylic, 2% polyester
6-oz. (185-yd.) skeins

Imagine (Article #780)
Worsted-weight yarn
80% acrylic, 20% mohair
Solids: 2½-oz. (222-yd.) balls
Multicolors: 2-oz. (179-yd.) balls

Jamie® Pompadour (Article #890)
Sport-weight yarn
85% Acrilan® acrylic with Bounce-
    Back® fibers, 15% rayon
Solids: 1¾-oz. (196-yd.) skeins
Prints: 1½-oz. (170-yd.) skeins

Jiffy® (Article #450)
Chunky-weight brushed acrylic yarn
100% Monsanto acrylic
Solids: 3-oz. (135-yd.) balls
Multicolors, Heathers, and Dusty Grey:
    2½-oz. (115-yd.) balls

Kitchen Cotton (Article #760)
Worsted-weight yarn
100% cotton
Solids: 5-oz. (236-yd.) balls
Multicolors: 4-oz. (189-yd.) balls

Microspun (Article #910)
Sport-weight yarn
100% microfiber acrylic
2½-oz. (168-yd.) balls

Wool-Ease® (Article #620)
Worsted-weight yarn
Solids, Heathers, Twists, and Prints:
    80% acrylic, 20% wool
Sprinkles, Wheat, Mushroom, and Rainbow
    Mist: 86% acrylic, 10% wool, 4% rayon
Glitter and Multicolors: 78% acrylic,
    19% wool, 3% polyester
Frosts: 70% acrylic, 20% wool, 10% nylon
Solids, Heathers, Twists, Sprinkles,
    Wheat, Mushroom, and Rainbow Mist:
    3-oz. (197-yd.) balls
Glitter, Multicolors, Frosts, and Prints:
    2½-oz.(162-yd.) balls

Wool-Ease® Sportweight (Article #660)
Sport-weight yarn
Solids, Heathers, Prints, and Twists: 80%
    acrylic, 20% wool
Wheat and Mushroom: 86% acrylic, 10%
    wool, 4% rayon
White/Multi: 78% acrylic, 19% wool, 3%
    polyester
White Frost: 70% acrylic, 20% wool, 10%
    nylon
5-oz. (435-yd.) balls

Wool-Ease® Thick & Quick (Article #640)
Chunky-weight yarn
All colors except Wheat: 80% acrylic, 20%
    wool
Wheat: 86% acrylic, 10% wool, 4% rayon
6-oz. (108-yd.) ball

Woolspun (Article #370)
Thick-and-thin textured yarn
63% wool, 26% acrylic, 11% polyester
100-yd. skeins

ORDERING INFORMATION:

Lion Brand Yarn is widely available in retail
stores across the country. If you are unable
to find Lion Brand Yarn locally, you may
order it by calling 1-800-258-9276 (YARN)
or by visiting the Lion Brand Yarn Web site
at www.lionbrandyarn.com.

PHOTOGRAPHS

Ralph Anderson: Front cover, 2, 4, 5, 6,
13, 19, 24, 30, 37, 46, 54, 62, 67, 73, 80,
83, 86, 95, 101, 103, 106, 109, 117, 121,
122, 126, 128, 132.

Jim Bathie: 11, 15, 29, 43, 44, 49, 51, 71,
92, 98.

Brit Huckabay: 14, 17, 21, 22, 23, 28,
32, 34, 36, 40, 53, 57, 61, 63, 64, 65, 68,
70, 76, 77, 78, 84, 85, 87, 89, 90, 94, 102,
107, 114, 125, 127, 135.

PHOTO STYLING

Kay Clarke: 11, 15, 23, 29, 34, 43, 44,
49, 51, 57, 61, 64, 68, 71, 77, 78, 92, 98.

Catherine Fowler: 2, 4, 5, 6, 13, 19, 24,
30, 37, 46, 54, 62, 67, 73, 80, 83, 86, 95,
101, 103, 106, 109, 117, 121, 122, 126,
128, 132.

SPECIAL THANKS

A very special thank-you to **Adina Klein**
of Lion Brand Yarn Company for her
invaluable contribution to project
development.

Additional thanks to the following
people for their assistance:
Lauren Caswell Brooks
Ed Glaze
Cathy Mathews